CALLINGS

Also by Dave Isay

*Listening Is an Act of Love: A Celebration
of American Life from the StoryCorps Project*

Mom: A Celebration of Mothers from StoryCorps

All There Is: Love Stories from StoryCorps

*Ties That Bind: Stories of Love and Gratitude
from the First Ten Years of StoryCorps*

CALLINGS

| *The Purpose and Passion of Work* |

DAVE ISAY

with Maya Millett

PENGUIN PRESS

NEW YORK

2016

PENGUIN PRESS
An imprint of Penguin Random House LLC
375 Hudson Street
New York, New York 10014
penguin.com

ISBN 978-1-59420-518-7

Printed in the United States of America
1   3   5   7   9   10   8   6   4   2

DESIGNED BY AMANDA DEWEY

DEDICATED TO EVERYONE WORKING TO FIND AND FOLLOW

THEIR CALLINGS. MAY YOU LIVE WITH COURAGE ALWAYS.

"Tell me, what is it you plan to do
with your one wild and precious life?"

—*Mary Oliver*

CONTENTS

| II |

GENERATIONS

| III |

HEALERS

| IV |

PHILOSOPHERS

| V |
GROUNDBREAKERS

CALLINGS

The idea for *Callings* came four years ago. It was around Mother's Day, and our StoryCorps book about moms had just come out. I was lucky enough to go on *The Colbert Report* to talk about it. My wife was pregnant with our second child at the time. The day after I did the show, we had an appointment with our beloved ob-gyn, Austin Chen.

I adored this woman from the minute I met her: tiny, fierce, mercilessly blunt, brilliant at her work. I knew a little bit about her. I knew that she worked ferociously hard. I knew that she biked everywhere she went—to her office, to the hospital in the middle of the night to deliver babies. I knew that she had made the commitment to personally deliver the babies of every single one of her patients, which meant she was on call twenty-four hours a day, 365 days a year. She told me that she had tried to leave town only once in the twelve years since she'd started her practice, to say good-bye to her father, who was dying. But while she was there, a patient called to say she was in labor. Dr. Chen left so she could meet her patient at the hospital. She was not able to be with her dad when he died.

Dr. Chen had seen me on TV the night before our appointment, and as we were leaving she said, "I wish I had done something important enough with my life to be on *Colbert*." I was stunned. I told her that as far as I was concerned, if you took everyone who had ever been on the show and added up everything they'd accomplished, they wouldn't hold a candle to her. She shook her head and ushered me out of her office.

Later that day I had a meeting with our publisher to figure out the next StoryCorps book. I told her about my conversation with Dr. Chen earlier in the day. We looked at each other and we knew we had our answer—the book you now hold in your hands: *Callings*. (A year later, I recorded a StoryCorps interview with Dr. Chen about her work, which you can read on page 142.)

I am thankful every single day that I was lucky enough to find my calling as a young man. I was twenty-two years old, headed to medical school, when I fell into public radio completely by accident. The moment I pressed the button on the tape recorder to begin my first interview, I had an overwhelming sense that I had found what I was going to do for the rest of my life. A few weeks later I withdrew from medical school. It was a terrifying decision, but one of the best I've ever made. My fate was sealed.

The theme of work threads throughout StoryCorps' dozen-year history. The legendary oral historian Studs Terkel, whose most famous book is *Working: People Talk About What They Do All Day and How They Feel About What They Do*, cut the ribbon on our first StoryCorps booth in Grand Central Terminal. "We know who the architect of Grand Central was," shouted a stone-deaf ninety-one-year-old Studs at the launch. "But who were the brick masons? Who swept these floors?" Studs implored us to celebrate these stories, and we've devoted ourselves absolutely to the task since that day.

Work, Studs wrote, is about the search "for daily meaning as well as daily bread, for recognition as well as cash, for astonishment rather than torpor; in short, for a sort of life rather than a Monday through Friday sort of dying." *Callings* is in many ways a 257-page proof of Terkel's proposition.

Many of the sixty-five thousand conversations recorded in StoryCorps booths across America over the past dozen years have dealt with the subject of work, and we've dug deep into our archive to cull the most powerful stories and the wisest words from those interviews for this collection. The following pages are filled with the stories of everyday people who have found—and often *fought*—their way to doing exactly what they were meant to do with their lives. Many of these stories have never been broadcast or published before. They are the voices of men and women of varied age, geographies, and backgrounds, driven by a fire from within to find meaning in their work—ignited by hope, love, or defiance, and stoked by purpose and persistence.

Listening has always been at the heart of StoryCorps' mission. And, as you'll read in these stories, finding what you're meant to do with your life has a lot to do with careful listening—to that quiet voice inside that speaks to who you really are. As the writer and teacher Parker Palmer wrote in his book *Let Your Life Speak,* "Before you tell your life what you intend to do with it, listen for what it intends to do with you."

Building StoryCorps has been the most difficult thing I've ever done—replete with moments of abject terror and doubt. But it's also been the most ridiculously rewarding and nourishing work of my life. I can't imagine doing anything else. One of the original employees who helped launch StoryCorps described the work as: "Hard work. Blood work. Love work." Which is an apt description for the work lives of so many who are fortunate enough to find their callings.

For those of you in search of your calling, consider yourself warned: this pursuit takes discipline, resilience, enormous sacrifice, and tremendous hard work. At those moments when the fear creeps in and you're unsure of where to go or what to do next, remember to trust your instincts always. Relentlessly follow your curiosity, allow yourself to be led by what truly moves you. And don't compromise your values—ever.

Whether you've found your calling, are on the journey, or

have lost your way, may the heroes of this book—whether astronaut, ballpark vendor, or ob-gyn—help remind you of the importance of finding meaning in your work. May their words help give you the strength to listen to that still, small voice inside—that voice which can help you discover the work that you were born to do.

—*Dave Isay*

AUTHOR'S NOTE

The following stories were edited from transcripts of Story Corps interviews that typically run forty minutes. We aimed to distill these interviews without altering the tone or meaning of the original sessions. At times tense and usage were changed, and a word or two was added for clarity. We did not use ellipses to indicate omitted text; in the following pages ellipses indicate speech trailing off or a pause in speech or conversation.

Words and phrases that read well are not always the strongest spoken moments, and the reverse is also the case. As a result, a story may vary from audio to print.

Participants gave permission for their stories to be published in this book, and each story was fact-checked.

| I |

DREAMERS

JOHN HEYN, 56, TALKS WITH HIS UNCLE HERMAN HEYN, 83, A STREET-CORNER ASTRONOMER.

John Heyn: Uncle Herman, what did you think you were going to be when you grew up?

Herman Heyn: Well, I wanted to be a scientist, but I had learning disabilities. I have a bad memory for lists of words; I couldn't remember rules of English grammar, or spelling lists and vocabulary lists. . . . I just wasn't a good learner.

But when I was in the eighth grade, my science teacher, Miss Wicker, drew the Big Dipper on the blackboard one day and said, "Go find it tonight." So I went out and found it that night and thought it was totally beautiful. I got hooked on astronomy from that very moment.

My mother used to say, "You can spell Andromeda, but you can't spell anything they want you to in school. What's wrong here?" *[Laughs.]* But stuff I really wanted to learn for myself, I could concentrate real well and learn a whole lot—no learning disabilities there. So at the age of thirteen or fourteen, I started getting books out of the library and did a lot of reading on astronomy.

Eventually, around age fifteen, I leaned on my father to get me a telescope, and I've just been with it ever since. Astronomy—it's just *me*. Some people like trees, some people like birds. For me, it was always stars. It's just a part of my nature—in my genome, so to speak.

John: You inspired the family to become stargazers. Growing up, I don't recall we ever had a telescope, but I remember you giving us maps of the constellations. They were these glow-in-the-dark charts, and we would kind of take them outside and hold them up in the sky and try to match up the constellations.

Herman: Well, you know, I've always had what I call an "education bone," and what you just described is an example of it. I got a degree in elementary education in general science, but I decided I didn't want to teach in a classroom because of my learning disabilities. I couldn't remember kids' names. I couldn't even get organized enough to write them down.

And so I went into various kinds of jobs—lab tech, sales, and so forth and so on—and each time I'd start a new job I'd say, "I'm going to stay with it. I'm going to get benefits and vacation and retirement and raises," but three years later I wouldn't be able to stand it anymore, and I had to get out of there and get another job. I had so many jobs, I can't even make a list of them all, but it would be a very long list.

And then, one beautiful night in November 1987, the moon was up, Jupiter was up, and I had nothing on my schedule. And so I decided, *Heck, I'm going to take my telescope out on the street and invite people to look at the stars.* And as I was walking out the door I said, "Oh, I'll take a tip hat with me, too, and see what happens."

I set up the telescope in Fell's Point, and I had people looking at the moon and Jupiter. I think that first night I made ten dollars. Then I went back the next night and made forty dollars, and I moved the hat a little closer. And I said, "Well, if I can make money at this, maybe I can do it full-time."

And that's really how I got started as a street-corner telescopist. I became very serious about it. I went out every possible night, till two or three o'clock in the morning sometimes, and set up the telescope, even in cold weather. Sometimes I'd have to recruit a passerby to take my wrench and unscrew the bolts on the telescope when I wanted to go home, because my fingers were too stiff.

When I set up, I have a sign on the front of the telescope that says, "Tonight Saturn and its rings. HAV-A-LOOK!" That's my trademark: *HAV-A-LOOK!* Then, as people are passing by, I'll say, "Have a look, folks. The moon: an awesome view through my telescope!" or "Have a look, folks. Tonight the rings of Saturn. A chance of a lifetime!"

John: You've said that when you started, there were people who thought what they were seeing was not real. Can you explain that?

Herman: Well, when you look through a good telescope at the moon or, say, Jupiter or Saturn, it's quite amazing. And probably 99 percent of all the people that look through my telescope had no idea that these things looked that way. Especially with Saturn, people would say, "It's not real!" I used to go through five different ways of trying to prove to them that it is, and finally I gave that up. Now I just say, "If it looks fake, it's in good focus," and people accept that. *[Laughs.]*

I really enjoy sharing my love of the celestial sky with anybody and everybody. I say the best part of my life is being out there with a telescope, and then it's downhill from there. *[Laughs.]* And you know, underneath it all I'm a scientist. All the information I give out about the planets and the moon is scientifically correct. There have been people who have looked through my telescope and taken up astronomy themselves, bought their own telescopes, joined an astronomy club. Somebody even told me they named their boat *Saturn* after looking at it through my telescope. And all of that makes me feel like this is worthwhile.

John: How many years have you been doing street-corner astronomy?

Herman: I just finished my twenty-seventh year. By actual

count I've been out on the street 2,637 times—I keep a log. Each night when I go home I write down what we looked at, any special things that happened, any friends who visited, and put a number on it.

I'd say my street telescoping is the same today as it was on day one or two—the reactions of the people, the way I respond to people. It's like being in a Broadway show that has a long run. The only thing that's changed is I've gotten older, and I haven't had quite the stamina that I had when I was younger. I used to pick up the telescope and carry it for hundreds of feet, but now I'm lucky if I can carry it ten feet.

Back in 1997 when the Hale-Bopp comet came around, I was in a write-up in the *Baltimore Sun* paper. They asked, "How did you get started in astronomy?" and I talked about Miss Wicker in the eighth grade. At that point I didn't know if Miss Wicker was dead or alive. But she saw the article, called me up, and I actually met with her at her retirement home.

I visited Miss Wicker a couple of times after that, and we became good friends. And when she died, I was one of the eulogizers at her funeral. I said that one of the questions I get most often when I'm on the street is, "How did you get started in astronomy?" And I always say, "Miss Wicker's class." I talked about how often her name is still out there, being circulated in the public.

Over the years, I've been hoping that somebody would

come along and say, "I got my degree in science" or "I got my PhD in astronomy having first looked through your

telescope," but it hasn't happened yet. Maybe there are others out there that I don't know about. I'm still hoping.

RECORDED IN BALTIMORE, MARYLAND, ON DECEMBER 8, 2014.

JOHN MAYCUMBER, 42,
TALKS WITH HIS GIRLFRIEND,
BARBARA ABELHAUSER, 44,
A BRIDGETENDER.

John Maycumber: Jacksonville, Florida, is a place of many bridges. Sometimes when I pass over one, I see that little shack nearby and I wonder, *Who is that person in there, and what do they do?*

Barbara Abelhauser: Well, that would be me. I've been a bridgetender for eight years. First job I've had in my whole life that I don't mind getting up in the morning and going to work.

For fourteen years I worked as a state employee, and I was *miserable*. I would wake up in the morning and dread going in. I just wasn't happy with the whole pantyhose and office politics kind of thing. Then I woke up one day and I was like, *Life's just too short.*

I had always thought what a Zen kind of job bridgetending must be, so I looked into it. I thought I was only going to take a little break from corporate society—maybe a year or so—but here I am years later. The pay's horrible, the benefits are worse, but the job itself is great. I love it.

The bridgetender house is just a tiny little space; it's smaller than your average walk-in closet. Mainly it's just a place for me to sit, and there's a console with all the buttons that open the gates and raise the span. The bathroom and the kitchen are in other buildings across the street, which makes things fun when it's pouring down rain and you have to go to the bathroom.

I can't even stretch my arms straight out to the side inside the house, but it's got windows all around, and I have the most gorgeous view in the entire city. I mean, executives who make hundreds of thousands of dollars a year do not have my view.

The Ortega River Bridge, where I work now, was built in 1927. And I think of the fact that twenty-four hours a day, seven days a week, for all these years there's always been someone sitting in that room—always. I wonder what the person in 1927 was like, and who the first woman was.

There seems to be some sort of a rite of passage with the teenage boys in the neighborhood: you have to egg the tender-house at least once. And when you're in there and you're not expecting it, it sounds like mortar fire. It scares the living life out of you!

But you know, the bridge is a place of community. We get

joggers, we get people walking their dogs, they go on dates and they propose—people consider these bridges as parts of their lives.

John: You must see a lot of things that the rest of us miss.

Barbara: I've been sitting in the same exact spot for these eight years, and I see the passage of the seasons. I see the alligator that hangs out below my window in the summer, and when she lays her eggs and they hatch, I hear the barking of the baby gators. There's manatees and the dolphins that come by. There's a night heron that sits just below my window all night long every night, except when the algae bloom. And the sunsets and sunrises are like snowflakes—there's no two that are exactly alike.

People don't realize that bridgetenders exist. We're like this invisible force in the world. People'll walk past us and say the most intimate, private things, and we hear them, and they don't even know we're there. So you get this little tiny snapshot of people's personal lives they don't even realize that they're giving you.

I get to know people that I don't talk to but that I see every single day. There was a fisherman that used to come through the bridge every morning like clockwork. I never knew his name, but we'd always wave, so we had a connection even though we didn't really know each other. And one day he came through, I waved, and then I found out in the news that maybe ten minutes later, while he was on his boat heading out to fish, he had a heart attack and passed away. He was on the boat alone, and his boat washed up on the shore of the river. So I was the last person who saw him alive. That really makes you think. Makes you appreciate.

John: You do have some very heavy responsibilities as a bridgetender, too.

Barbara: As Zen and relaxing as the job is 90 percent of the time, there's this 1 percent that can be white-knuckle terror, because the last thing you want is for somebody to get hurt. People have died on drawbridges. People have lost limbs. One of the most frustrating things that I find is that people assume that I'm asleep in the tenderhouse, but I have never once fallen asleep. I take this job seriously.

It's kind of funny—on my bridge the average opening only takes four minutes, but a lot of people will get impatient and do a U-turn and go the long way around, which will wind up taking them longer. This four-minute interruption in their lives is apparently a very big deal to a lot of people—it amazes me. But then other people get out of their car and take pictures of the view and enjoy it while they're waiting. So it's a mixed bag.

I'm getting paid to stop and look—that's the thing I think I love the most about this job. I know it's the same manatee that comes back every year, because I know his scars. I have this love-hate relationship with a crow that likes to attack me as I'm walking off the bridge, and I talk to him.

I took a pay cut for this job, and that was hard. But you know, I could get hit by a bus tomorrow, and if that happens I want to have woken up that day and not thought, *Ugh, I don't want to go to work.* So it really is worth it to me. Most people don't stop to smell the roses, but I get to smell the roses eight hours a day. It's amazing.

RECORDED IN JACKSONVILLE,
FLORIDA, ON DECEMBER 6, 2009.

FORENSIC ARTIST
SHARON LONG, 74,
TALKS TO HER COLLEAGUE
STEVE SUTTER, 57.

Sharon Long: I had been working four and five jobs a day, seven days a week, for twelve years. I worked at the Dairy Queen, I cleaned a dentist's office, I painted apartments, I worked as a secretary in different departments at a university—and I was worn out.

I had raised my two daughters as a single parent, and when I was enrolling my oldest in college, I said, "Geez, I sure wish I could go to school." But I was forty, and I thought I was too old. The lady filling out my daughter's financial aid paper said, "You can! I'll help you." And I thought, *Whoa—OK!* So I started college, and enrolled for an art degree.

I had to take a science class, but I told the adviser, "I'm not any good at science. So what can I take?" And they said to take anthropology. Didn't even know what it meant. *[Laughs.]* So I went home and I looked it up, and I thought, *The study of mankind—that sounds interesting.* So I took physical anthropology and *bang!* I decided what I wanted to be when I grew up.

While I was doing my sculpturing degree, I branched into taking all these anthropology classes, and I got really into forensics. My anthropology adviser, Dr. Gill, said, "You know, you're an artist. Why don't you try making faces?" And he encouraged me to try facial reconstruction. He gave me a skull and said, "Let's see what you can do with it."

When I brought it in, I didn't know if it was any good or what, but Dr. Gill said, "Man, that guy looks alive!" He took some pictures and showed some of his friends from the Smithsonian, and next thing I knew, he called me and said, "We have a team from the Smithsonian going to Easter Island. Do you want to go?" They wanted me to make molds of skulls, since you can't ship human remains.

I didn't ever believe in myself, but they all encouraged me, and it felt good. I started getting one skull after the other— and it's just been a succession of skulls ever since.

The human skull is one of the hardest things that you can possibly mold and cast, because it's very intricate and there are so many little facets. It takes almost as long to prepare the mold as it does to build the face. I spend twenty or thirty hours just making the skull mold and cast.

Then, when I prepare to build the face, I keep the skull in front of me for a while, just looking at it and forming it in my mind. I kind of meditate about their life, and depending on their age, I try to go by when I was that age. I've researched the time period—what they would have been wearing, where they lived, what they ate—and I try to think about them as a person like me, because they were, once upon a time. They loved people and families and ate and drank tea with their friends. I don't talk out loud to these people like some kind of wacko, but I am thinking to myself, *OK, help me out here. Guide me a little.*

I get totally psyched in to what I'm doing, just like people must do when they write music or paint a painting—anything artistic. It doesn't even seem like much time goes by. You forget to eat, you forget to get up, you forget to drink water. Everything just goes into suspension. And then fifteen hours later, I have a face.

I really don't know how I do it; it just comes out the tips of my fingers. But I do observe *a lot*. I watch people pretty closely in restaurants, in airports, people I work with. If you look at people closely, you'll notice one eye might droop a little more at one side, or the nose will be up a little higher on the other side. I just read every little thing in their face.

Steve Sutter: I remember talking to you once, and you started staring at my forehead, and you said, "Can I feel your brow ridge?" *[Laughter.]*

Sharon: Aren't I awful? With friends I can say, "Can I poke on your face a little?" But I can't really do that at the airport. *[Laughs.]*

All the skulls I've done have been joys, but it can be really hard on me. I've done forensic work for murder victims, people being tortured, and I've had nightmares. You try to eliminate those things from your mind, especially because if I think about them in pain during their dying moments, their faces will come out looking like that. It stresses me out—big-time. Because it isn't just some dead person's face you're making; you're actually bringing them back.

I've done something like eighty-six skulls, and I have a file on every person. I look back and I think, *I can't believe I did all that.* But now I'm tired—my hands hurt. I've got arthritis. I know what they're doing with facial reconstruction on the computers now, and they have state-of-the-art equipment. It's amazing to see. What I do is a thing of the past, and I think technology is moving so fast that I can't keep up.

But I will miss it. I just felt like I was trying to help someone tell their story, and that was exciting. Every time I did a skull, I thought, *This is probably the last one I'll ever get.* But people kept calling me. It just seems like it's all been a big long dream.

RECORDED IN LARAMIE, WYOMING,
ON MARCH 20, 2015.

NBA REFEREE MARAT KOGUT, 31, TALKS WITH HIS DAD, LEON KOGUT, 63.

Marat Kogut: Growing up, I played basketball at the rec center by us, and when I was about fifteen I sprained my ankle. I couldn't really run, so I asked my coach if I could referee the practice instead. I was terrible—had no idea what I was doing—but it was a lot of fun. And so I started volunteering at games on Saturdays and Sundays.

Most kids grow up dreaming that they could hit the game-winning shot of a championship. I was the one that said, "I want to be the referee that blows the whistle and says the basket was successful." Being a player, sometimes you may have to sit on the bench. But I always wanted to be right in the middle of the action—and when you're a referee, you're the one controlling the game.

Leon Kogut: When you told me someday you're going to be

a referee, I said, "Yeah, sure." But it was your goal, and so it became our family goal. Then one day you came from school and said, "Dad, can you give me two hundred dollars to get a course for referee?" Remember? It was the first investment in your future.

Marat: When I took the written exam to become a licensed referee that November, about 115 people took the test. Thirteen passed, and I was one of them. Most of the people were in their thirties, forties, and fifties, but I was sixteen.

In high school, refereeing at all these rec centers on weekends was a great way to earn some extra income, but I wasn't doing it for the money. I was doing it because I really loved it.

Leon: I used to drive you to every game, because you didn't have a driver's license at that time.

Marat: Right, I only had a referee license. But you have always been supportive, no matter what I said. If I told you I wanted to be a ballet dancer, you would say, "Oh, good!" Mom, on the other hand, was totally against it. Her main concern was to marry me off. "Who's going to take a guy who's going to be a referee?"

Leon: Yeah, she wants to see you as a doctor, as a lawyer, you know. But I always remember when you asked me, "How many lawyers do you have in this country, Dad?" I said, "Maybe three, four million?" "How many doctors do we have in this country?" I said, "About six, seven million doctors?" And then you asked, "And how many NBA referees are there in this country?" I said, "I don't know." You told me, "It's about sixty. And I'm going to be one of them."

I'm never going to forget that. You knew you were going to be there. Since that, I said to your mom, "That's it, don't bother him anymore. He's going to be an NBA referee."

Marat: My first official NBA game, my partner gave me the ball, and I'm the one that got to throw it up to start the game. I was so nervous up until I finally released the ball in the air; then all my training just clicked in. I was like, *This is just another game between two teams. I'm here, I earned my spot. Let's go to work.*

Leon: I remember your first game in the tri-state area, everybody came to the game—the whole family went to support you. I'm a barber, and a lot of customers from my shop went to that game also.

Marat: It was a hell of a turnout! And they filled up a whole section. During the last time-out, I saw a whole bunch of them start screaming, "Marat! Yeah!" My partners were looking at them like, "Wow, all those people are here for you? You have more fans than the players do!" *[Laughs.]*

I just finished my second season, and I'm exactly where I want to be right now. I got hired at thirty, and I'm planning on doing this for another thirty years.

Leon: Everybody told me, "Your son is in the NBA? No, it's impossible." I say, "Yes. He is." Now all the customers in my shop, everybody ask me about you. And everybody's looking for your games to watch, then the next day they call me up, say, "Oh, Leon, I saw your son!"

Marat: I still go to your barbershop to get haircuts, and every time there's a customer, you say, "Hey, this is my son," and the first thing that comes out of their mouth is, "Oh, your father always talks about you."

Leon: Of course! I'm proud of you, that's why. I watch all the games on TV—I never miss even one game yet. If you work in the west and the game start ten o'clock at night and finish one o'clock in the morning, doesn't matter. I still watch to the last minute.

We came to the United States from Kiev when you were seven days old. And I choose your name, Marat, because I just

have a feeling, *This name going to bring you lots of success.* So when I see my son is in the arena, and you blow the whistle there . . . it's incredible—the dream's come true.

RECORDED IN NEW YORK, NEW YORK,
ON JUNE 5, 2011.

AEROMEDICAL FIELD TESTER
ALTON YATES, 73,
TALKS WITH HIS DAUGHTER,
TONI YATES, 46.

Alton Yates: I was the second of seven children, and my mother passed in 1953. My dad, who was a civilian employee at Naval Air Station Jacksonville, was trying to raise the seven of us by himself—and it was nearly impossible. I knew that as soon as I finished high school, I was going to have to find a job so that I could help him take care of the family.

Toni Yates: How did you know that your dad needed your help?

Alton: Well, it was obvious. After he came home from work, he did these extra things to try to make enough money to take care of us. He had this little machine that he used to roll cigarettes, and he'd roast peanuts and then put them into little bags and sell them to the sailors on Ashley Street.

I just couldn't stand to see him continue to struggle, and I had to do something about it. But this was after the war, and we were children of the Depression, so to speak. There weren't any good-paying jobs for youngsters just out of school. If you couldn't find a job or were not going to college, the next best thing was to join the Armed Forces. So I decided to serve in the Air Force.

Toni: Do you remember the day you left?

Alton: Oh, I do. It was very difficult to walk out and see my brothers and sisters by themselves. But I knew they were going to be all right as long as my dad was there, and my monthly allotment check was coming home to help support them. I was a little bit apprehensive about what lay ahead for me in the Air Force, because I had no idea, but I was ready.

I was assigned to the Aeromedical Field Laboratory in New Mexico, and when I arrived, I learned that a call had gone out for volunteers for a little-known program to determine the effects of space travel on the human body. Keep in mind, this was 1955, and we had no NASA—there was no space program. But they needed volunteers who would serve as human subjects in these tests, and I was very fortunate in that I worked for Colonel John Paul Stapp, who was in charge of conducting all of those tests and recruited me into the program.

When I walked into the laboratory the first day, Colonel Stapp looked up at me, and he said, "I've got something I want to show you." He took me out back to a little short track they had, called the "Daisy Track." He said, "You think you might be interested in riding that?" I said, "Riding?" I had no idea what he was talking about, but I was interested in doing anything he asked me to do.

And so I became one of the "human guinea pigs," as we were later known, who rode high-speed rocket sleds. The Aeromedical Field Laboratory, in cooperation with the Ford Motor Company, developed an instrument that we called the "Bopper" sled, which was used to test the effects of abrupt deceleration on the human body. We flew high-altitude balloons, and we did the first studies that resulted in automobiles now having seat belts.

Toni: What was it like to be in the sled?

Alton: Oh God—oh! It was like if you drove an automobile at a hundred miles an hour and ran it into a solid stone wall. When the sled took off, it was almost as if everything in your body was being forced out through your back. And then when it stopped, it was like all of your insides were trying to be pulled out from the front of your body.

Let me tell you, there was something about the group of volunteers we had out there. I remember one, Captain Eli Beeding, rode the sled one day, and his body absorbed more than forty g's. When they took him off the sled, he was like a dishrag. The rest of us riders were right there, and we saw what happened to him, but we were anxious to get strapped into that seat, to go on to conduct the next experiment. I was nineteen when I did my first ride, and I did those tests more than sixty-five times.

In addition to the rocket sled rides, there were all kinds of devices that were built to test different kinds of stresses on the human body. We went up to Johnsville, Pennsylvania, because they had a huge centrifuge up there, and they strapped us into it, and we rode that thing at high speeds. Fortunately with that one, you had your hand on a little trigger, and the minute you started to black out, of course your body would go limp and your hand would come off the trigger, so that would stop the centrifuge.

Toni: Were you ever scared?

Alton: You know, there's always a little bit of fear of the unknown. You're apprehensive about what's next—but scared? No. Excited? Yes. Ambitious? Yes. A little foolish? Sure.

I was able to do things during that time that the average American citizen didn't have the opportunity to do. This was a very select group of men. And if you consider the fact that a kid just out of high school from Jacksonville, Florida—no college education whatsoever—would be afforded the opportunity to do something like this, it's almost unbelievable!

Toni: Did your dad know what you were doing?

Alton: He didn't know initially, but my dad always knew that if there was anything dangerous to be done, I was the one who would be doing it. *[Laughs.]*

About four years later, I got word that my dad was ill, and

they didn't know how long he would live. So in October of 1959, I left the Air Force to come home. We got a chance to talk, and he told me how proud he was. But more than that, the men he worked with told me that he would tell them about me and what I was doing and that sort of thing. *Ebony* magazine had published an article with pictures of some of the rocket sleds that I had been riding, and I'm told that when my dad got a copy of that magazine, he took it everywhere he went, and he was just as proud as he could be.

I think that's one of the things that made me feel really great about what I was doing—making my father proud was something that I always wanted to do. And I was able to do that before he passed away, in January of 1960.

Toni: So what was it like for you the day that man went into space?

Alton: I can see it in my mind's eye now. When I heard the countdown, a warm feeling came over my body. I could see myself there with them all the way. We had accomplished the objective: to safely put a man into space. Even to this day, every time there is a liftoff I think a little piece of me lifts off with each one of those missions.

RECORDED IN JACKSONVILLE,
FLORIDA, ON NOVEMBER 19, 2009.

CARL McNAIR, 57, REMEMBERS HIS BROTHER, ASTRONAUT RONALD McNAIR, WITH HIS FRIEND VERNON SKIPPER, 57.

Ronald McNair lost his life on January 28, 1986,
when the NASA Challenger space shuttle exploded just seconds
after liftoff, killing him and the rest of the crew.

Carl McNair: We knew from an early age that my brother Ron was different. When he was nine years old, Ron decided to take a mile walk from our home down to the library—which was, of course, a public library, but not so public for black folks, when you're talking about 1959 in segregated South Carolina.

So as he was walking through the library, all these folks

were staring at him, because it was white folk only, and they were looking at him and saying, you know, "Who is this Negro?" *[Laughter.]*

He found some books, and he politely positioned himself in line to check out. Well, this old librarian says, "This library is not for coloreds." He said, "I would like to check out these books." She says, "Young man, if you don't leave this library right now, I'm going to call the police!" He just propped himself up on the counter and sat there and said, "I'll wait."

So she called the police and subsequently called my mother. The police came down, two burly guys, and say, "Well, where's the disturbance?" She pointed to the nine-year-old boy sitting up on the counter. One of the policemen says, "Ma'am, what's the problem?"

So my mother, in the meanwhile, she comes down there, and she's praying the whole way: "Lordy, Jesus, please don't let them put my child in jail!" My mother asked the librarian, "What's the problem?" The librarian said, "He wanted to check out the books. You know that your son shouldn't be down here."

The police officer said, "Why don't you just give the kid the books?" And my mother said, "He'll take good care of them." Reluctantly, the librarian gave Ron the books, and my mother said, "What do you say?" He said, "Thank you, ma'am." *[Laughs.]*

Ron did exceptionally well at school, and he was very good in science and math. During his junior year in high school, his chemistry professor told him about a summer institute for math and science, so he went three hundred miles or so from home to participate in this program. He met a professor there who said, "The highest academic level you can go is PhD, and young man, I think you should shoot for it." And Ron says, "That sounds like a pretty good idea, sir. I'll get a PhD." And he went on to get a PhD from the Massachusetts Institute of Technology. Then, when NASA was looking for astronauts, here he was with a PhD in physics.

Ron went on a space flight in February of 1984. When he went out in space and he looked out at the world, he saw no lines of demarcation. It was a world of peace, he said. And two years later, he took his last flight on the space shuttle *Challenger.*

You know, as youngsters, a show came on TV called *Star Trek.* Now, *Star Trek* showed the future, where there were black folk and white folk—all kinds of folk—working together. I looked at it as science fiction—that wasn't going to happen, really. But Ronald saw it as science *possibility.*

He was always someone who didn't accept societal norms as being his norm. That was for other people. In Ron's own words, he was the kind of person who "hung it over the edge." He'd go as far as he could, then go one step beyond that.

Ron was a country boy from segregated, small-town South Carolina. Who would dream that he could become an astronaut? But it was his time. And he got to be aboard his own starship *Enterprise*.

RECORDED IN ATLANTA, GEORGIA, ON MARCH 18, 2007.

The library in Lake City, South Carolina, was renamed the Dr. Ronald E. McNair Life History Center on January 28, 2011, twenty-five years after Ron's death.

LIBRARY ASSISTANT
STORM REYES, 64, TALKS TO HER
SON, JEREMY HAGQUIST, 44.

Storm Reyes: Working and living in migrant farmworkers' fields, the conditions were pretty terrible. My parents were alcoholics, and I was beaten and abused and neglected. I learned to fight with a knife long before I learned how to ride a bicycle.

When you are grinding day after day after day, there's nothing to aspire to except filling your hungry belly. You may walk down the street and see a row of nice, clean houses, but you never, ever dream you can live in one. You don't dream. You don't hope.

When I was twelve, a bookmobile came to the fields. I thought it was the Baptists, because they used to come in a van and give us blankets and food. So I went over and peeked in, and it was filled with books. I immediately—and I do mean *immediately*—stepped back. I wasn't allowed to have books, because books are heavy, and when you're moving a lot you have to keep things minimal. Of course, I had read in the short periods I was allowed to go to school, but I'd not ever owned a book.

Fortunately, the staff member saw me and waved me in. I was nervous. The bookmobile person said, "These are books, and you can take one home. Just bring it back in two weeks." I'm like, "What's the catch?" He explained there was no catch. Then he asked me what I was interested in.

The night before, an elder had told us a story about the day that Mount Rainier blew up and the devastation from the volcano. So I told the bookmobile person that I was nervous about the mountain blowing up, and he said, "You know, the more you know about something, the less you will fear it." And he gave me a book about volcanoes. Then I saw a book about dinosaurs, and I said, "Oh, that looks neat," so he gave me that. Then he gave me a book about a little boy whose family were farmers. I took them all home and devoured them.

I came back in two weeks, and he gave me more books, and that started it. By the time I was fifteen, I knew there was a world outside the camps, and I believed I could find a place in it. I had read about people like me and not like me. I had seen how huge the world was, and it gave me the courage to leave. And I did. It taught me that hope was not just a word.

When I left, I went to vocational school, and I graduated with a stenographer's degree. Then, when Pierce County

Library had an opening, I applied and was hired. I got to spend thirty-two years helping other people make a connection with

the library. I have a deep, abiding commitment to them. Libraries save lives.

RECORDED IN TACOMA, WASHINGTON,
ON MARCH 7, 2014.

SCIENTIST DR. DOROTHY WARBURTON, 78, TALKS TO HER SON, BOB WARBURTON, 51.

Dorothy Warburton: My father was a chemical engineer who worked for the pulp and paper industry in Canada. He always wanted a boy and didn't have one, and so he used me to talk about science.

I remember him sitting me down and telling me how the atom bomb worked when it first went off. And I thought, *Well, he knows how it works; why is it such a big secret? [Laughs.]* He also bought me a chemistry set at a very early age and taught me how to use it. The worst thing I ever did was make soap that blew out of the tube and slid down the kitchen wall, and my mother was very annoyed because she could never get rid of that streak. *[Laughs.]* My father didn't really have much expectation that, as a girl, it would ever lead to anything. He truly didn't understand—and never made me understand—that I could really have a future in science.

Then, when I was about fourteen or fifteen, I won an essay contest, and for the prize I got a lot of books about women scientists, which made me think maybe this could happen. I went into university studying biology, but I remember I bought a book on touch-typing and I taught myself to type, because I had this notion that someday I could perhaps be a *secretary* to a great scientist, and I could sneak in in the evenings and work in the lab. That's how naive I was.

After graduating, I set out to write a master's thesis. But about halfway through the thesis my professor said to me, "You know, this is really a PhD project, so why don't you just stay another year and we'll give you a PhD?" I think when he said that my work was good enough for a PhD, I began to have some belief in my own abilities. I had reason to keep trying and pushing, and I ended up with a PhD in human genetics in 1961, when I was twenty-five.

But when my husband got a job teaching at Columbia University in New York, I just kind of tagged along. It was only because of economic circumstances that we had to find a job for me as well. So I got a position as a research associate in the OB-GYN department.

I realized that physicians were not interested in the problem of miscarriage very much at all. Even simple things like, *How common is it?* had not really been studied. Also, obstetricians tended to think of miscarriages as something that women wanted to forget as quickly as possible, whereas women were interested in it, wanted to talk about it, wanted to know the reason.

So I started interviewing patients as part of my research. The doctor would say, "She's not going to want to talk to you. She's too upset." But when I would actually explain that I was trying to do research on what happened to them and I wanted to ask questions, the women were more than willing to spend hours with me.

No one had really shown that miscarriage was anything to be concerned about. Doctors would just say something like, "God gets rid of the abnormal." And yet in the women's hearts they knew it was something to be concerned about. And what helped a woman more than anything was to have someone who was interested in the problem and trying to find out something about it.

Columbia at the time I came there was not exactly woman-friendly. There were very few female professors, and women did not move forward very rapidly. I remember once complaining to the chairman of the genetics department that there weren't any women on the committees in the department, and he made me chairman of the refreshment committee—which meant I organized the coffee and donuts. Put me in my place, right? [Laughs.]

Also, I had four kids at a time when most women who had

children did not work. I came home every night and washed diapers. I think about those days and I'm not sure how I ever got through them! But I was lucky to have a husband who helped with all the kids and was willing to take on household chores; we've always shared those things.

I was also lucky in that the director of the hospital did support me, and in 1969 I was able to start the Genetic Diagnostic Laboratory at Columbia, which did chromosome analysis on women with reproductive problems. It was among the first in the country.

The work can be stressful. Often you're telling patients bad news. People are in pain, and it's not nice to see that. On the other hand, there are times when I'm telling them good news or news that's better than they thought it would be. I have a whole bunch of letters from parents who send me pictures of their babies and say, "Thank you for saving my baby," because they'd heard from their doctor or from somebody else that it was going to be very bad, and the baby was born and it was perfectly normal. They give me credit, and that's nice, but they really shouldn't, of course.

I have had one big tragedy in my life, which is that I lost my oldest child when she was twenty-two. I still can't talk about it without a catch in my voice. That was more than twenty years ago, but I don't think anybody who's ever lost a child ever forgets it. It's with you a lot, and it's very hard. I think it has perhaps left me with a little more understanding of other people who've had these kinds of tragedies in their life. I know what not to say and what to do to be helpful. And that's probably a good thing.

My life isn't what I thought it would be—certainly when I was younger. But I'm pleased with the way things turned out. I never quite imagined achieving what I've achieved. In fact, I'm not even sure I still imagine it. So I'm going to continue to do good work for as many years as I can. And I don't intend to stop until I have to.

RECORDED IN ENGLEWOOD, NEW JERSEY,
ON OCTOBER 30, 2014.

DENTIST THOMAS McGARVEY, 71, TALKS TO HIS FRIEND AND PATIENT ANNE BRANDE, 40.

Thomas McGarvey: My father was an immigrant from Ireland, and he come along in Iowa and picked up this farm girl who was from a family of thirteen. They traveled all over the dang country, and they had children all the way along as they were working their way across. We were thirteen, too: seven boys and six girls.

Mom and Dad ended up in Rock Springs, Wyoming, in the coal mine. My youngest brother, the thirteenth child, was nine months old when my dad got crushed in a mine accident. I was six, and the saddest day of my life was that day. Mom had all the children and an eighth-grade education. It was just one of the worst things that could happen.

I remember people telling me things like, "Your dad was a good man, and God wanted him." And that began a war with me and God. As a child I said, *Who in the hell is God? Gonna take my dad away?*

Anne Brande: So then what was your family environment like?

Thomas: Everybody went to work when my dad died. We were required to bring home half of what we made and give it to Mom to manage the house. Since twelve years old I've been totally financially responsible for my life. There was never talk of college—only high school. My mother promised my father that she would get us all through high school, so that was the main deal.

I worked as a mechanic at a filling station, and that's where a Navy recruiter got me. I went in and took some tests, and he said, "You could go to the Hospital Corps." And I said, "Does that involve bedpans and stuff? No, I don't want that." He said, "Dental technician," and I have to tell you, my intuition just knew. I said, "I want that. I will take that." I was only seventeen, so my mom had to sign the paper, and then off I went.

I really excelled in the dental assistant courses, and it was the first time that I felt that I had a direction. I was just enthralled with mechanical dentistry and dental assisting. I knew every instrument and what they used them for. And I saw everything the dentists did when I assisted them. When they did my wisdom teeth when I was eighteen, I knew every instrument they picked up. They wouldn't give me a mirror, but I knew what steps the guy was doing. Just watching the dentists

I thought, *I can do that better than they're doing it*. I mean, that's pretty brazen for an eighteen-year-old. I didn't have the college preparation, but I didn't think it mattered.

I knew then that no matter what was going to happen, I was going to become a dentist. I've never had such a burning desire. When I wrote my mother and I told her, she thought I was from Mars or something, because we had never talked like that in our family. We didn't have those kind of sights.

When I applied to school, I told them, "This is why I want you to accept me into your dental school: I am going to be a dentist whether you accept me or not." And I got in.

As I look at my life, there have been a lot of happy moments: when I got married, when I had my first child—and when I had my second, third, fourth, and fifth ones. But the happy moment that stands out the most in my life is the day I got accepted to dentist school; I literally leaped five feet in the air.

By the time I had graduated, I already had my practice planned in my head. I knew what equipment I was going to get, and I had already contacted the dealers. And when I started the practice, I had so much energy, you cannot believe it. I worked twenty-five hours a day—and it was just exciting. I was a workaholic, but it really was not work. I was absolutely having a creative, fun time with all of the patients I got to meet, and the different challenges of their problems.

Some of these cases are difficult, and they are challenging, and you've got a lot of responsibility with them. But they've got redeeming rewards every moment of every day. And I want to fix things so that they last. I have been a practicing dentist for forty-four years now, and I've had so many interesting people come in. I've tried to learn lessons from every one of them. I'm not sure I've learned easy, but they come to show you how to think different.

Here I am, seventy-one years old, and I've got as much drive for dentistry as I had when I was twenty-five.

You know, life lessons are our attitudes. So get whatever it is you want in your heart, and in your gut. And once you've got it, don't ever let go.

RECORDED IN LARAMIE, WYOMING, ON JULY 12, 2008.

| II |

GENERATIONS

FIREFIGHTER DEKALB WALCOTT JR., 60, TALKS WITH HIS SON, DEKALB WALCOTT III, 27, ALSO A FIREFIGHTER.

Dekalb Walcott Jr.: Our family was poor, and many of our ancestors didn't have a very good education. They came from the South and were farmers, cotton pickers, and so on. They all made their own clothes, they grew their own food. I don't think my mother or father finished high school. I had four sisters, and everything was short: food ran out, never had a new car, things like that.

I wanted to be an attorney, so I started out in college with plans of going to law school. But my focus just wasn't on school; it was getting a decent employment where I could have a family, and take care of that family.

You know, there's a saying: you shoot for the stars, and if you land somewhere in between, you're still in good shape.

And when I came on the fire department in 1978, it provided an opportunity for me—and my family—to move up in society. My life changed.

But being very honest, I never had the aspiration to be a fireman. When I first came on the job, I was thinking, *What the hell did I get myself into?* It was kind of a rude awakening for me. You know, you get to a building and you can't see in the windows because of the smoke that's billowing out. You open the door and the smoke and heat meet you at the door. But I really grew up on the fire department.

I remember standing in the doorway of my firehouse one day, looking out of the window, and I said, "I'm going to have a son, and he's going to come on this job, too. And it's going to be all good."

Dekalb Walcott III: I was a kid who wanted to grow up and be just like his daddy. Back in the nineties, when Michael Jordan was really famous and everybody wanted to be like Mike? Well, Mike was good—but *me*, I wanted to be like Dekalb Walcott Jr. You were my Michael Jordan.

I remember one day Mom said, "We're going to visit your father at work." I was already in the car before she could finish the sentence. When we got to the firehouse, you were about to go on a call, and you said, "You wanna come with me?"

Dekalb Jr.: You were eight years old. I was trying to wait until you were ten, but I felt that you could handle it.

Dekalb III: I jumped in the truck with you, and my eyes got big from the moment the siren went off. It was just like, *This is the life I want to live someday.* You know, I spent a lot of time drawing pictures of fire trucks—I could remember exactly the way the engine was laid out, just based on memory. And when I'd come home from visiting you, I'd take my little fire trucks and I'd be rolling them around the house, imitating siren sounds, pulling up to imaginary fire scenes and raising up the ladders.

I also had a godfather and a bunch of family friends who were firefighters, so all I ever wanted was to be a part of that. People always thought I would change my mind. You know, kids grow up saying they want to be like their dad, and it's usually just a phase that they go through. But I never strayed off that path.

I finally did get to become a Chicago firefighter when I was twenty-one years old. I remember the day I graduated from the academy, after all the training and studying—I felt like that was my championship round right there. It was the Bears winning the Super Bowl, the White Sox winning the World Series. I mean, any magic moment you can think of, that's how I felt—and then some.

I was the last one to walk across the stage to grab my badge, and I could feel the energy in the air. People knew me from when I was a child, because they knew you, and they were all talking to me as I was walking past. And then I remember hugging you for a really long time, thinking, *I made it!*

When I first got on the force, I was assigned to Engine Company 116, the busiest engine on the South Side. We're in and out, doing twenty-plus calls a day, and barely getting any sleep at night. Of course, it wasn't easy. I always had to keep my eyes and ears open. I remember when I was a kid you used to tell me, "Shut up and listen; pay attention to everything around you." Because with this job, just when you think you know it all, something else is going to hit you.

One time, we had an early morning fire—about five o'clock in the morning. We pull up to the building and see one of the worst types of fires you can have. I'm in the stairway throwing water around, and it's getting hot really quick—the heat and steam is coming right at me. Eventually we were able to get the roof open, and we ventilated the place. When I got back to quarters, I looked in the mirror, and I saw the skin peeling off my face. And I was like, *This is a lot worse than I thought it was.*

Dekalb Jr.: But you managed what you were faced with. And you know, when you put yourself in harm's way to help someone else, that's really what makes you a good fireman. And big picture: you put that fire out.

I remember I received a phone call that night. They said, "He's got some burns, but he's OK. He put the fire out all by himself, and everybody here's proud of him." Moments like that, it's heaven on earth for a dad. I'm very, very proud of who you are and who you turned out to be.

When you first came on the fire department, I saw your confidence grow; I saw your self-esteem grow. From when you were a young child, I used to ask you periodically, "How do you feel about yourself today?" Some days, they were good; some days, they were OK; and some days, they were bad. But as soon as you came on the fire department, I said, "Well, how do you feel about yourself now?" And you were grinning from ear to ear, like, "I feel great!" And that means everything to me.

Dekalb III: I've been on the force for six years now, and I love every bit of it. I'm so proud of being a second-generation fire-fighter. And knowing our family history—the struggles in the past and what it took to get here—makes me realize that ev-erything I've gotten up to this point is a blessing. And I'm definitely look-ing to pass this torch down to my son, if I'm fortunate enough to have one. I wouldn't have it no other way.

RECORDED IN CHICAGO, ILLINOIS,
ON APRIL 8, 2014.

FUNERAL DIRECTOR DON BYLES, 65, TALKS WITH HIS DAUGHTER AND PROTÉGÉE, MACKENZIE BYLES, 25.

Don Byles: Byles Funeral Home was started by my grandfather back in 1904. My father ran the business after my grandfather died in '52. I think I was in junior high when I figured I was going to follow in the family footsteps. You know, I just didn't think too much about doing anything else. And now you will be the fourth generation of the Byles family line.

Mackenzie Byles: When Vanessa and I were kids, I remember we did little funeral services for all of our hamsters. You dug the hole on the side of the house when Snickers died. And then when Vanessa's hamster died, we kind of buried him right next to Snickers in a shoebox. I should've known then!

Don: That was the beginning for you, but your sister didn't want anything to do with the business.

Mackenzie: Yeah, she barely comes in the door. *[Laughter.]* I was in high school when I really started to think that maybe this was something I wanted to do. I would come to the funeral home and visit you, and I was always just around and interested. And then I started working here part-time in the summers.

Don: Now I know when I was growing up and hitting the dating pool, I got some reactions when people asked what I did. *[Laughs.]* Have you had any problems?

Mackenzie: I'm single now, so maybe I just don't know that it's affecting my dating life. *[Laughter.]* But I definitely think it's intimidating. They'll either just walk away or they'll want to sit down and know everything when I'm really trying not to think about work.

Did I tell you about the time at school when I was at orientation and this girl asked me what my major was? When I told her, she didn't say anything, and then she turned around and walked away. I got scared that my whole college experience was going to be people not wanting to be my friend because I work in a funeral home and they thought I was weird.

Don: What do you think the hardest part of your job is?

Mackenzie: People don't realize that it's a 24-7 thing—especially kids my age. When I'm out at a bar and I'm like, "I got a call and I have to go in to work," they're like, "Right now? It's eleven thirty at night!" I'm on call every other night and every other weekend, so I don't get much freedom.

I am also aware that some people probably think that because I'm young, I don't know what I'm doing. I get mistaken for a secretary more times than I would like to.

Don: But I think some people also find it to be a breath of fresh air that they don't see just us old guys; they see a nice young lady—different voice, your bubbly personality.

Mackenzie: We deal with people of all ages, from newborns to a hundred-plus. And it makes me very conscious that anybody could be gone at any time. I find myself getting teary-eyed sometimes, especially when it's someone my age or younger. I'll have to walk away, because I don't want people to see me. I'm supposed to be there to help them.

Don: Yeah, I think probably the toughest one for me was when we had a father and three children who all got killed in a house fire, and there was a surviving wife and child. It was very, very difficult, because that isn't the way it's supposed to work. Kids are supposed to bury their parents, not parents bury their kids.

Mackenzie: Dealing with family strife is also hard. You know, everybody has different personalities—

Don: And family dynamics can come into it, too. Most of the time, dealing with the families is harder than dealing with the bodies. Death can really start people going. We've had calling hours where one part of the family's sitting on one side of the room and one part is on the other side. I've even been here when the police had to escort somebody out.

Mackenzie: Embalming or dressing the body doesn't faze me anymore; I just do what I need to do. But when there's a fighting family, or someone's yelling on the phone, I'm afraid that I'm not going to know how to handle it.

Don: Well, it's a tough thing sometimes, because you've got to listen to everybody. But having somebody come up and say, "Thank you. Everything was the way we wanted it to be. You made everything easy"—that makes it all worthwhile.

Mackenzie: I've still got a lot to learn before you retire—I've got big shoes to fill! I mean, everybody that I've ever spoken with at the office talks about how great you are. I admire that. I've never been nervous about working here, other than letting you down. Are *you* nervous for me to take over?

Don: No! I'll teach you everything I can and get you all squared away before you throw me out the door. And I'm positive you won't let me down. They'll be talking about you before too much longer.

RECORDED IN NEW LONDON, CONNECTICUT, ON JULY 30, 2013.

LEDO LUCIETTO, 80,
TALKS WITH HIS DAUGHTER,
ANNE LUCIETTO, 45,
A MECHANICAL ENGINEER.

Ledo Lucietto: My father, Luigi, was an engineer, and he worked at that profession for years.

Anne Lucietto: And when he retired, he came and hung out with you guys at the shop—

Ledo: He'd make the tools, or he'd say, "Let me run the machine." He didn't want to work heavy anymore; he just kept us occupied. And you were at the shop many, many times. You'd say, "Hey, Nonno"—that means Grandpa—"what is that? What are you doing? How do you make that?" *[Laughter.]*

When you were five years old, you started to ask me many, many questions, too. First it was, "Can a girl be an engineer?" And I said, "There is no question why they should not be." And from there on, it was, "How do you do this? And how do you do that?" It was constant. And if I did not know the answer, I would hunt and search in order to get some information so I could tell you to the best of my ability.

Anne: What other things did I do as a kid that made you think that I wanted to be an engineer?

Ledo: Well, if you remember, we'd go to the zoo, but you wanted to go to the Museum of Science and Industry. We had to drive a good hour in order to get to it, but we went there as many times as we could.

You were just interested in taking stuff apart—like little toys and things. And then I'd take you with me to the shop, and you'd watch the machines run and ask me a lot of questions: "What is this, Daddy?" Or you'd take the starter out of a car: "What's that for?" *[Laughter.]*

Sometimes you'd take something apart and I'd sit there and wonder what in the world did you do. Then you'd say, "Daddy, fix."

Anne: And then when you fixed it, I was watching real careful so I could take it apart and put it together myself next time. Did you ever notice that I always followed you around the shop, watching? And it wasn't just at the shop.

Ledo: I thought there was a magnet hooked up to me and to you. *[Laughter.]* But you weren't just mimicking me; you wanted to be there and learn what you could.

I did say you could be an engineer of any sort—you could become a doctor or you could become anything that you wanted to do—it is just a matter of putting it in your mind and doing it. And I said, "Once you start, don't give up." You know how many people said to me, "What do you want to send her to college for? She's only a girl. They're only good for making babies"? But I always told them, "That's my money and I'm going to worry about it." And you did it—you became a mechanical engineer.

Anne: And my first day on the job, I really felt like Nonno was with me, and that it was meant to happen.

Ledo: Well, it *was* meant to happen.

Anne: So you don't worry about me anymore, huh?

Ledo: No, I do worry—but I'm very happy you're successful. Sometimes I tear up with joy. And my father, that poor

guy would break into tears, too, he'd be so happy for you. I'm very proud.

RECORDED IN BALTIMORE, MARYLAND, ON NOVEMBER 7, 2008.

TOOL AND DIE MAKER
PHIL KERNER, 49.

*Tool and die makers produce tools and machine parts
used in the manufacturing industry.*

Phil Kerner: I was born and raised here in Erie, Pennsylvania. You'd find that to be a very common thing in Erie—that people don't leave. Everything you need is right here. For many years, the manufacturing jobs were so good and so high-paying, there was no reason to *have* to leave.

Growing up in Erie in the 1960s in the boom years, with the amount of money that was around town, anybody could go out and start a tool and die machine shop and do very well. My grandfather, Edward Kerner, had taught all his boys the tool and die making trade in the basement of his home on Cochran Street. And two of them became shop owners: my uncle Eddie and my uncle Ronnie.

Now, Uncle Eddie started a shop back in the late forties, early fifties, called Kerner Tool & Die Company. And my father, Frederick—known as Fritz—was the foreman there. He was a very hard worker; I remember hearing the razor blade running at five o'clock each morning, and my father came home pretty tired at five thirty every night.

Tool and die shops have their own unique odor to them, and I always remembered the smell of ours. Most shops have these things called EDMs—electrical discharge machines— which use a very distinct oil. If you walk into a shop with an EDM machine in the back of the building, you'll smell it when you come into reception. I also remember the smell of the hand soap that you squirt out for the guys in the shop; it had a little grit in it to clean your hands.

I spent so much time at the shop just to see my dad and uncle. It was the center of my universe. My uncle Ed was a tremendous businessman and a lot of fun. My father was a smart, quick-witted guy, but he was wound pretty tight. We always believed that he had horrendous experiences in World War II. I know his ship was torpedoed five or six times and they were ordered to abandon ship each time, but somehow they always got out of it. So he was a pretty stressed-out type of guy, and I think it did him in very young. He died at forty-eight, in 1969. And then my uncle Ed died six months later, when I was nine.

After that, my life just kind of crashed. The shop eventually was sold and burned to the ground a few years later. Then my mother remarried and we moved to the other side of town. I learned really quickly that whatever I wanted in life I was going to have to go out and get myself.

I decided to go to a technical high school and take up tool and die drafting, and I really fell in love with it. To this day I love to draw, and my printing is impeccable because we had to print a thousand *a*'s, a thousand *b*'s, a thousand *c*'s, until we got it right.

Then I went to college for about a year, and it just drove me nuts—I couldn't wait to work. So I quit. I said, *I think what I really want to do is be a tool and die maker.* My brother introduced me to a guy who had started his own shop, and he gave me my first job in the trade, at nineteen.

I hadn't been in a tool and die shop since I was nine or ten. And I remember when I walked into the place, I knew the smell like *that*. It felt like my heritage, like where I should be. So after that, I apprenticed, and then I spent years in the trade trying to make sure I knew as much as I could before I started my own shop. I was very anxious to resurrect the family name, and in July 1991, when I was thirty-one years old, that's what I did.

Somebody told me that a scrap metal dealer in town had ended up with a machine called a Deckel, which I really needed for the shop, and I worked out a deal. Well, the first thing I do when I buy a used machine is I wash it down, which really helps you get to know it a little bit. And as I'm cleaning, I find this giant *K* on the side of the machine, and it said, "KAMCO"—Kerner Accurate Machine Company—which was a little division of my uncle Ed's shop. Very few machines made it through the fire that burned down his shop, but that machine did, and after all these years, I got it. That to me was a sign. I felt like it was my uncle Ed saying, "Here, this was one of mine. Go get 'em!" We built a lot of molds with that machine.

It was really exciting to grow and build the company, especially in those first few years when you're trying to do everything on a shoestring. But things started to get tougher in the late nineties. I noticed the customers were now being driven by their purchasing departments, who said, "No, it's got to be cheaper." And the little guys really couldn't afford to compete. And so in about 2002, I realized I was not going to make it.

The closing of my shop was a crushing day. And you know, I did feel like a failure. But probably the worst part of it was standing there alone, with no support network. So my wife and I started an organization to help small business owners right here in Erie not have to go through what I went through. There's a hundred of them getting together every month, referring business to each other—helping each other. So in the end, I'm thankful.

My father was a tool and die maker. My uncles were tool and die makers. My brother was a tool and die maker. And surprise, I became a tool and die maker. But you know what? I have four sons, and they're not going to be tool and die makers. It's a global economy now, and it's easier to get work done all over the world. I never thought that they could ever do that with the tool and die work, but they did. It really did hurt, and it's still hard for me to drive by the building. It's been six years, and I don't go down that street too often.

RECORDED IN ERIE, PENNSYLVANIA,
ON AUGUST 2, 2009.

BRICKLAYER BARBARA MOORE, 62, TALKS WITH HER DAUGHTER, OLIVIA JUNE FITE, 33.

Barbara Moore: When I was in high school I thought I was going to be a teacher, but there was no money for college. So right out of high school I worked in an office—but a couple of hours behind a desk and I was falling asleep. I had many, many jobs by the time I turned twenty-one. And then I started looking into the bricklayers' apprenticeship program.

Money was the greatest incentive. An apprentice in the bricklayers' union started making $3.50 an hour—twice as much as I was making—and bricklayers were making *$8.50* an hour! It seemed like an awful lot of money to me. And I wanted it. When I got anywhere near the bricklayers' office, I would stop by and say, "How's my application doing?" And at some point I guess they realized I wasn't going away.

Olivia June Fite: And when you did get the apprenticeship, what did your family think about it?

Barbara: Well, my mother was very afraid for me, because she thought I was going to get hurt. I think my father, like most men, doubted that I could actually do it, but that didn't stop him from asking me to do masonry repairs on *his* house. *[Laughs.]*

At first, a lot of the guys didn't think I should be there. But I very much challenged anybody saying that, because I believed in the bottom of my heart that I had a right to that job. And I could really hold my own.

Because most of the guys were bigger than me, I would always volunteer to work in these really tight areas. It helped me hone my skills—and because I was willing to do that, the other guys would say, "I'll take that corner with the heavy block." So it was a good trade-off.

Once the guys saw I was serious about staying, and that I was actually a very good bricklayer, I won their respect and I made many dear friends. I remember in the first or second year of my apprenticeship, I was working with this guy Tony. He was a World War II vet who had a metal plate in his head from the war. He had headaches all the time, and he was a pretty unhappy person. But I think he had a daughter about my age, so he kind of took a liking to me. He was a really old-school guy, but he was willing to work with me when a lot of other people did not want me as their partner. And he taught me everything he knew. That meant a lot, because having a woman on the job was something he probably couldn't even imagine previous to that.

When he passed away, his daughter called me and said that he wanted to leave me his tools, and I went out and picked them up. If you're getting tools from the bricklayers that have gone before you, that's a sign of respect.

Olivia: What was it like for you to work when you were pregnant?

Barbara: Oh, it really wasn't that different. I mean, my midwife told me that I could do whatever I normally did, and since I normally laid brick, I continued to do that until my eighth month. When I was laying block, I couldn't run off the scaffold every time I got morning sickness—I would have gotten fired. So I would just throw up inside the block and keep working. *[Laughter.]*

Olivia: The block that you already laid?!

Barbara: Oh, worse things have gone in those blocks than my vomit, believe me. *[Laughter.]*

Olivia: Out of all the many buildings that you worked on, is there a favorite?

Barbara: Well, I can look out my window and see many things that I worked on. I renovated one of the oldest basilicas in the country—the whole building was built out of masonry.

It's just a beautiful building, and when you get a job like that, that's the best kind of experience.

But sometimes you're building a warehouse and all it is are twelve-inch blocks that weigh about thirty to fifty pounds apiece and there's nothing about it that's interesting. Because it can be a very repetitive thing: you spread mortar and you put down the brick or the block and then you spread more mortar and you do the same thing. Day after day, hour after hour. That day you're just there for the money.

Olivia: But I can't even really remember a time that you came home and said, "I'm going to quit; this is too hard." You barely seemed physically tired, even after working in the cold for sometimes ten hours a day. You actually helped me have a lot more confidence about my own physical abilities. I always thought, *Well, my mom only weighs 115 pounds and she lays bricks for ten hours a day, so why couldn't I lift this crate or drive a truck?*

One of my favorite childhood memories is going to sleep while you took your rough, calloused hands and gently rubbed my back. I loved it! And I learned how to massage your hands at a very young age—and sometimes I would paint your fingernails, too.

Barbara: Not that a manicure lasted very long! *[Laughs.]*

Olivia: No, but treating your hands was always just a nice thing I could do for you. Now you've got these knobby knuckles after years of working with them, but they're a lot softer now that you're retired.

Growing up with a mother who was strong both physically and emotionally has had an incredible impact on who I've become. I knew bricklaying was something that made you financially independent, and I remember being fourteen and very eager to get my work permit and get my first official job—not just babysitting, but actually working and getting a paycheck and a bank account. I was very excited to be a worker.

And when I went to college, I always felt like I was doing it for the both of us, because I knew you didn't get a chance to go. You helped me go to school and paid the tuition by laying bricks. I mean, how do you ever repay someone for that?

Barbara: You have shown me your appreciation—always—so I don't feel like I need to be repaid.

You've never given me a lick of trouble and have always inspired a great deal of pride in me. And whatever I did, I don't

feel like it was a sacrifice at all. It was always something that I wanted to do for you.

RECORDED IN BALTIMORE,
MARYLAND, ON JULY 20, 2014.

ENGINEER AND ENTREPRENEUR NORAMAY CADENA, 34, TALKS WITH HER DAUGHTER, CHASSITTY SALDANA, 16.

Noramay Cadena: The summer I was thirteen, my mother took me with her to the bungee cord factory where she worked. A bell rang in the morning, and that meant it was time to start. All these people sat on both sides of a really long table. Along the table were big piles of plastic hooks. I spent eight hours a day putting hooks into bungee cords, making piles, tying the piles, and delivering them to a different station.

What I remember most is my mom being proud that her daughter was there, but at the same time not wanting other people to talk about me, which is why she kept saying, "Sit up straight! Work faster! Don't talk! You're not doing it right!" I remember the bells that rang for breaks. I remember the lines to heat up your lunch. I remember thinking, *I don't like this place, and I don't want to work here. I don't even like it that my mom works here.*

That first summer working in the factory was enough to show me what my life would be like if I didn't do anything different.

In high school, I was a great student. Someone came to my school, pulled me out of class, and said, "Hey, you're good at math, and you're good at science. Have you ever considered engineering?" I didn't even know what an engineer was, but that opened my eyes.

You were born the first month of my senior year. And I felt this pressure to make sure that I created opportunities for you that I didn't have growing up, so I knew I had to go to college. It would be hard, but I had no other choice.

I wish I could remember the day I made the decision that I was going to move three thousand miles away from home and raise a kid by myself at MIT. At no other time in my life have I been as brave as I must have been that day.

Chassitty Saldana: What were some of your hardest times?

Noramay: There were so many things going on at home that I wished I could help with, or times when my mom needed me and I just wasn't there. But I knew that the only way to help them, and the only way to help you and help myself, was to focus on this one thing that was going to make the biggest difference.

Every week at school, as hard as it was, I kept thinking, *If I can only get through this week, next week will be better.* By taking it a week at a time, I made it. And I made it in four years, even though no one thought I would.

I finished at MIT in 2003 with a bachelor of science degree in mechanical engineering. I worked for six years before going back to MIT, where I got an MBA and a master's in engineering systems.

I remember feeling like Superwoman during both of my graduations. Seeing how happy my parents were, and how proud they were, gave me this huge sense of hope for what you would do. It felt like the beginning of a new life for all of us, and it was a beautiful feeling.

Throughout my career, I worked to improve the working conditions in factories. Every time I toured a factory, looking at safety and ergonomics, I thought, *Let me put myself into the shoes of the person sitting here,* because I've been there. Sometimes the height of the table can make a big difference. The type of chair can make a difference. How far people walk to deliver or pick up work can make a big difference.

Both my parents continue to do factory work, and it's like a reminder in my ear that the people working there are real people, and that we all have a responsibility to do what we can to help other people. That's part of what makes us human.

Chassitty: Seeing you go through so much, I've learned that you should always continue, no matter what other people say, and prove them wrong. I'm sure a lot of people said you wouldn't graduate, but you did. You graduated high school. You graduated MIT. And you graduated MIT again.

I see people who are stuck in situations and they can't get out. But you showed me that anything is possible. So when I do find my career, I want to make sure that it's something I love and I don't feel stuck. I want to go to work and be happy.

RECORDED IN LOS ANGELES, CALIFORNIA, ON JULY 13, 2015.

Chassitty Saldana (*left*) and Noramay Cadena.

SCULPTOR OLGA AYALA, 57,
TALKS TO HER EX-HUSBAND,
EFRAIM AYALA, 61,
ABOUT HER MOTHER,
ARTIST RAMONA CRUZ.

Olga Ayala: My mother, as wonderful and strong as she was, she was bipolar most of her life. When she was a little girl, her mother committed suicide, and that traumatized her. I've always had a very close relationship with my mother, and with that, I was always very protective. She was very timid, and I'm not. I came out more like my father, this real fiery personality. So whenever my father would go out somewhere, he'd say, "Take care of your mother"—and I took that literally. I felt that I was responsible for her.

We lived in a tenement building in El Barrio—East Harlem—and everybody knew everybody. We had a meat market on the block, and the guy that owned it had a big crush on my mom. His eyes would light up when he would see her, and she'd always get the best cuts. I remember when I was young, we were walking down our street, and there were these guys leaning up against cars, telling her how lovely her dress is and how she makes their hearts sing. My mom was a very modest woman, but she was a head-turner, she really was.

My mom also had wanted to be an artist, and she did have talent. But we were a traditional Puerto Rican household, and once she got together with my dad, they fell into the typical roles—the man saying, "Your job is to stay home and raise my children, to run the household." So she put what she wanted to do on the back burner.

When I was about five or six, I remember, one day she was doodling on a grocery list, and she drew a picture of Mickey Mouse. I mean a full-fledged Mickey Mouse, not a stick figure with little circles. I was totally flabbergasted. I thought she was like a god, you know? And I told her, "You have to teach me how to do that."

Once I showed an interest, that was *it*. When I didn't have to do schoolwork or chores, I was drawing. No piece of paper was safe around me. I was always getting in trouble at school, because instead of doing my lessons, I was drawing my teacher. I even had the nerve to go up and show the teacher the portrait I did instead of my work.

When parent-teacher night came around, the biggest complaint was, "She's not doing her lessons; she's drawing." My parents' answer to that was, "We need to buy Olga more paper at home."

Efraim Ayala: Did you ever make art with your mother?

Olga: We never created something together, but we did influence each other from the very beginning—from Mickey Mouse all the way until the time she couldn't create anymore. When we got a little older, she got back into art, and when she showed me something that she did, that would inspire me to create something of my own. But I always felt that she lived through me in a lot of ways. I went to the High School of Art and Design in Manhattan, and my mom told me that that was a gift, and that I should pursue it, because she was not able to.

When I decided to start selling my artwork at cultural events and street fairs, she would show up and just hang out for the whole day—just *thrilled* to be there. My mom was actually one of my first paying clients. I was like, "Mom, I can't take your money. If you see something you like, I'll give it to you." She said, "No, no, no, take it! I want to support you."

Efraim: Did she continue making art herself, before she passed away?

Olga: My mom had Alzheimer's and Parkinson's, and so until she could not physically create anymore, she created as much as she could.

The things my mom used to make, she created from her imagination. She wasn't the type of artist that would draw a portrait of somebody or a still life or whatever. In her apartment, when a ceiling or any surface had been repainted and it hadn't been scraped, you'd get these random patterns. She would look at them and see a face or a body or something, like looking at clouds and seeing shapes, and then she would sketch and paint that.

A lot of the things had to do with Puerto Rico, the Caribbean—lots of color. A lot of vibrant, tropical work. I think that she was drawing on the things she saw in her childhood that she didn't see in East Harlem.

Efraim: Is there anything in particular that you miss most about her?

Olga: I miss being able to share this gift she gave me. Whenever I tried a different art form or a different technique, I always shared it with her. So being able to go with a new idea or new medium and say, "Hey, Ma, I'm trying something new. What do you think?"—I miss that. And her unconditional

love. So, I look at my art as a living testimony to her. She was my greatest muse. *[Crying.]*

RECORDED IN NEW YORK, NEW YORK, ON JULY 24, 2015.

DR. LARRY MICHAELIS, 73,
TALKS WITH HIS DAUGHTER,
DR. LAURA MICHAELIS, 47.

Larry Michaelis: My father was a physician in Fort Wayne, Indiana, and he was a surgeon in the Second World War. When my father was away for the war, my grandmother spoke constantly and with great pride about him, and she always said her greatest desire would be for me to become a physician, too.

I can remember when I was four and five years old, my grandmother would have me try and cut the yolk out of a sunny-side-up egg without breaking it. Or she would give me little pieces of cotton and have me practice picking them up with a hemostat, a tiny clamp used to control a bleeding blood vessel. She'd say, "Since you're going to be a surgeon, you should learn to do that."

When my father returned from the war, I would often go with him to make house calls at night. If he got called to the emergency room, he would take me along and let me sit and watch him set fractures and sew kids up. And by the time I was about thirteen, he would take me to the operating room and let me stand at the end of the table and occasionally hold a retractor.

My father had textbooks of medicine and surgery and family practice at home, and after dinner I'd read the books and then ask him questions about it. It was a bit like an apprenticeship. So I knew by the time I was fourteen or fifteen that I wanted to be a physician and a surgeon. But I did not want to just be Steve Michaelis's son, in Fort Wayne, Indiana, who took over his dad's business—so I went off to medical school. I met your mother, who was a nurse, and then we went to the University of Virginia, where I took a residency in general surgery.

Laura Michaelis: I remember when I was a young girl, you used to take me to the hospital. We used to eat dinners in the hospital with all the other residents' kids at those long tables, with the tapioca pudding and the grilled cheese and the Jell-O and all the hospital food. I mean, when a swing hit me in the eye one time and you took me in to get stitched up, it was almost a thrill to have to get stitches, because I got to go to the hospital.

But when I decided to go into medicine after nine years of being a reporter, I remember you had some misgivings.

Larry: Well, I was worried that you had been jumping from

job to job, and that you might be trying to escape. But now I believe that being a physician was your destiny, and that you were just always fighting it. Now that you are a physician, you are so emotionally and spiritually fulfilled—I see it in you all the time.

From the time you were a little girl, you were always the most like me of the kids. And you were always determined to do something *your way*—and resistant to anybody else charting a path for you. So maybe part of why you fought it was because you didn't want to just be Larry Michaelis's daughter.

Laura: Sometimes I think that, but I also learned a lot more about you by becoming a doctor, because I felt what it was like to be attached to people who are putting their faith in you. I've realized that it's a blessing and a burden, and it's hard.

Larry: At an early age I realized my father didn't always have the emotional ties with patients that I wanted to have. He was just too busy; he'd see sixty people a day in his office and would spend five minutes with them, and he could be quite brusque. So I knew I didn't like that. I love to be with people, I love conversation; that's what keeps me going. And so I spent a lot of time trying to get to know my patients instead of just operating on them.

Losing a patient was personal—and it never got easier. I'd wake up in the middle of the night and call in because I was worried somebody was still bleeding and the hospital might not call me. And although I'm retired now, I just can't get away from being somebody's doctor. I still go and sit with good friends in their hospital rooms, and I tell them they better call a doctor to take care of this or that.

I believe that our family's nature makes medicine the right choice. My grandfather also wanted to be a doctor but never had the money to do it, so he was a pharmacist. But patients in town would come to Grandfather Michaelis's drugstore, and he would figure out what they had and mix up the drugs that they needed. So taking care of other people is the character and the spirit that has permeated our family for now four generations.

Laura: It feels like part of me, that I'm supposed to do it, that it's what I'm on the planet for. So thank you for being an example of what it is to take care of other people.

Larry: Well, as I say, I'm a much better physician now because of you. I think that you have incredible relationships

 with patients. And we've developed a bond and a friendship as physicians that I couldn't have with anybody else in the world.

RECORDED IN ATLANTA, GEORGIA,
ON DECEMBER 23, 2013.

FARMER JOHNNY BRADLEY, 72, TALKS TO HIS DAUGHTER, KATHY BRADLEY, 52.

Johnny Bradley: My first chore as a very small boy was to get plenty of firewood and stove wood. And as I grew a little bit older, I can recall coming home and taking the turning plow from Dad and breaking land with the mules.

It was a good, quiet life. I remember shortly after we got electricity to our house in 1942 or '43, we were privileged to get us a Philco radio where we could hear the Grand Ole Opry. All the neighbors gathered round, and we'd listen at it on a Saturday night. They would come in and just fill up the living room, and usually Daddy would have some peanuts or corn for them to shell or something, so we could plant them for seed. All of them just sit there until midnight listening to the radio.

Kathy Bradley: This was not free entertainment; Pa made them work for it.

Johnny: [Laughter.] Daddy always had an eye for getting done what he wanted done. And this just seemed like a real good way to do it.

Growing up, I knew we were sharecroppers. When I was about five, I started to pick what we call black-seed cotton. I took Mama's clothespin sack and went to the cotton field and picked about an eight- or ten-pound bag. And when we gathered our corn, we would take one wagonload and put it in our shed, and take the other wagonload and put it in the owner's shed. So we knew we had to share, and that we were working on another man's land.

I remember one time when I was probably twelve years old, this fella Mr. Bowling owned a store right on 301. And one day a truck come by and hit one of his hogs; looked like the hog was fit for nothing and was going to die. Mr. Bowling had an old black man named Dale that worked for him, and he told him that he could just have it. Well, Dale took that sow and got her back on her feet, and she made a big hog. But after Dale got the hog well, Mr. Bowling took it back and sold her. Dale didn't get a thing.

Right then it made me doubt very seriously that you could get too much justice. But that was part of the way it was back then, I guess. Being poor sharecroppers, we were about on the same level as Dale was. We were working for what the boss man would let us have—and that was not a lot. Dad didn't have a lot of education, but he worked hard and was a very good farmer. Still, we hardly ever had any money left at the end of the year. So I hate to say it, but I wondered if the owners were completely honest.

Kathy: You left the farm when you were about eighteen and stayed gone for a long time. And about the time I was ready to go to college, you went back and decided you wanted to farm for yourself. Why did you make that decision?

Johnny: After eighteen years in the insurance business, I had the opportunity to buy my uncle's farm, two miles from the house where I was born. I had left the country, but the country never got out of me. I liked that kind of life: out to myself, working the land, watching the crops grow. It had become a part of me—now even more so than it was then. I've just always wanted to be a country boy.

Kathy: But when the economy went horribly south in the 1980s, we all wondered if you would lose the farm.

Johnny: Well, it was a testing time. But my dad had taught me, even back when I was on the farm with him, he said, "Son, you can't whip a man that don't quit." And I just had no intentions of quitting.

I remember in one of those years, my brother, being an accountant, said, "Johnny, you went a hundred twenty-five thousand dollars in the red this year." But through perseverance, working with old equipment, and not spending a lot of money, we were able to manage and eventually pay for the land.

My dad said, too, "If a man knocks you down and you can't get up, bite him on the leg." And that's my philosophy for life. When a man quits, it's over. And when I quit, I want them to put dirt on me.

You know, if I could live in the house that I really wanted to live in, I'm living there. If I could have married the girl that I wanted to marry, I married her. If I'm in the occupation that I wanted to be in, I'm doing that. I borrowed a lot of money to go back to the farm, but I don't have to share it with the boss

man. I worked hard; I do my own figuring. And for that, I guess I'm pretty fortunate. And very pleased.

RECORDED IN SAVANNAH, GEORGIA, ON JANUARY 29, 2009.

ACTOR RICARDO PITTS-WILEY, 53, TALKS TO HIS SON, JONATHAN PITTS-WILEY, 22.

Ricardo Pitts-Wiley: I grew up in a little town called Sumpter, Michigan, out in the country. In my sophomore year, I got bused from a high school that had a large African American population—where I was comfortable—to a school where we were 2 percent of the population.

It was awful. I wanted to get out of there, so I did just enough to get by. But in my junior year, my theater teacher put me in a play, *Romeo and Juliet,* and I was the only black kid in it—and I caught hell. I caught hell from the white kids in this school and I caught hell from the black kids. And in some ways, it forced me to distance myself from both of them, because neither was willing to support what I wanted.

On opening night I came onto the stage with this kind of fake beard and this big, floppy mushroom hat made out of upholstery fabric that the director's wife had made, and everybody burst into laughter. It could've been a crushing moment in my life, but I said, *No, I'm not going to give in*, and I waited until the laughter died down.

I had this little, squeaky voice, and I just kind of dug in and begged for the spirit of Brock Peters, a black man with a big voice and muscles and *bad*, you know—*Porgy and Bess*, all that stuff. And I said, *I need that voice, Brock*—and he sent it to me. And when the voice came out, I *was* the prince. When I walked offstage after that opening scene, I said, *That's it! This is what I'm going to do for the rest of my life.*

I won a dramatic-arts scholarship to go to Eastern Michigan University. And after two years there, I said, *I got to see if I can do this.* I gave myself a year to see if theater was a real career for me. I wasn't getting a lot of work, but in the eleventh month of that year, Trinity Repertory came to town. I went to this audition, and I met the director; he was a big, tall white Texan. And I walked into his room with my little three-line résumé that still had my high school credit in there, and he looked at my résumé and just pushed it aside. We talked for a few minutes; then he said, "OK, come back at eleven o'clock and be ready to go to work."

I was twenty years old when I became a member of the company, and I found myself surrounded by these extraordinarily gifted, wonderful people. It allowed me to try things—

to write musicals with no musical background, to write plays with no literary writing background.

But probably for the first time in my life, I had a certain kind of insecurity about my ability. It was an odd feeling of waiting for somebody to shine a light on you, and you're exposed as a fraud who really doesn't have any talent. I spent a lot of nights going, *Why didn't I get all the gifts? Why can't I sing? Why can't I do certain things better?* But then I started to realize that you only get a portion of the gift, and if you're patient, the rest of it will come. I needed a music-writing partner, and one showed up one day. I needed great singers, and they just showed up. And with that came great friends, great people, incredible experiences.

You know, I always thought I'd make my mark on the world in the theater, that I would do something extraordinary—but your mother and I were determined to raise two strong black men. So while I wanted to work at the highest level and give back to my community, I couldn't even *think* about that until you walked across that stage and got that piece of paper.

Your brother has his law degree, and you just graduated from Yale. It looks like you're going to follow in my footsteps. I had discouraged you from acting, not because I didn't think you had the ability, but because if you don't find this path yourself, you will always be frustrated by trying to be somebody else. But I had to learn to relax and let you be who you were going to be. And I'm so proud of you.

Jonathan Pitts-Wiley: Well, I say this with bias, clearly, but you're a fine actor, and I think you would've done well. But instead, you made a decision to be a dad. You knew what you were sacrificing, and I don't ever look at you and wonder if you're content. You're acutely aware of your purpose. I'm jealous of that. I felt that you deserved to be recognized and to get a lot of admiration that I didn't see you getting, and that has always bothered me. But if recognition is a trade for being married for thirty-one years to the same woman and having kids that are doing pretty well . . . if that's the trade, well, we're all lucky.

Ricardo: What a wonderful, exciting, incredible time this is for all of us. I mean, we're the Pitts-Wileys! There's only four

of us in the universe, and I think families need to be on great journeys together, too. It keeps us all young.

RECORDED IN PROVIDENCE, RHODE ISLAND, ON JUNE 17, 2007.

GAYLE LAIN, 72,
TALKS WITH HIS WIFE,
SHERYL LAIN, 70, ABOUT HIS
FATHER, RED LAIN,
AN OIL RIG DRILLER.

Gayle Lain: Dad was from Rison, Arkansas. He's Irish and he had red hair, so all of his relatives called him Red. The Depression was going on and there were ten in the family, so Red and his brother Buck hopped a Cotton Belt train going north, so there'd be more for the rest of the kids. They went on up near St. Louis, where they heard there was work in the oil field and got jobs there. And then Dad met Mom, who was a farm girl, and they got married.

I was born in '42, and then World War II got to going. But Dad didn't go, because he worked in a critical industry: making gasoline for the war.

Sheryl Lain: What kind of work did he do on a rig?

Gayle: Well, Dad was a driller—that's the guy running the motors—and it's a hard job.

There's five men on a crew, and three crews. And the rig runs twenty-four hours a day. It's a lot of work, and there's never a stop. It continually drills deeper, deeper, deeper down—doing all kinds of things. But Dad was fast—and strong. He set records in the Salt Creek field. And his crew was tight. It was kind of like a basketball team: everybody had a job. And Dad was the head of the crew, kind of the captain of the team. He was proud of his team, and he liked his work—he was good at it. I think he had a sense of patriotism, because he was producing the absolute necessary product for our troops. And he had brothers that were landing in Normandy, and in the military all over the world.

Mother and Dad felt like pioneers because we were moving around all the time, chasing rigs, going to where the work was. We worked in Wyoming, then up and over Billings, Montana. We worked in Rangely, Colorado, and in Fort Collins. They loved the fresh air, seeing the country.

We always lived in a trailer house inside a trailer park. The trailer was small—eight feet wide, maybe up to thirty feet long—but we were proud of it and it was home. All of the people there were oil people. You'd see the same kids again and again in different towns where the well was drilling. Once, I moved to five different schools in one year.

Locals and oil field people didn't always get along just real good. I've been in a lot of fistfights. Usually you could talk your way out of it, but sometimes you couldn't. But it was an adventure. I liked the feeling of the pioneering spirit.

Sheryl: I know that life could be very hard, too. You've talked about the fact that snow went over the top of the trailer and frequently you couldn't even get out the doors.

For your mom, the first thing would be to get the kids in school, and then the next thing would be to find a church, and the third thing would be to find the county library.

Gayle: Oh yes, Mom was a good reader. We listened to Mozart on a record player in our trailer house. And we went to church every Sunday that we were in a town that had a church she liked: Presbyterian, mostly; sometimes Methodist.

Sheryl: Your dad was a storyteller. Can you describe what it would be like when he would break out with that look and you knew a story was coming?

Gayle: Everybody in the whole camp would gather around to hear his stories. For him, storytelling was acting, and he had a wonderful sense of humor. When his crew car came in from the rig, all the kids were happy to see it. And my dad would say, "Gayle, I want to tell you about what we did out at the rig today."

I remember once they had a blowout on the rig, and a guy was trapped up in the derrick and he couldn't get down. Everybody on the ground was saying, "Jump!" But he was afraid to, I guess. The fire got worse and worse, and he caught on fire and burned up. After a while, they got the fire out, but it had killed him. They needed somebody to go up in the derrick and see if they could recover his body, but nobody would go up there. They weren't sure how secure it was. So Daddy volunteered, and he went up and started trying to gather his remains, and the man's boot fell over one hundred feet to the ground. But it was completely burned; it was just ash. There was nothing hit the ground except the steel toe in his work boot. Dad said he was a good man, and that's about all you get. I knew from that point on that work on the rig was deadly.

We kept moving all over and wound up in Riverton, Wyoming. One day Dad was going to come in early from work and play catch with me, and I was surprised when he didn't come. I was twelve and growing into a pretty good athlete, and he was getting proud of the way I was playing.

That night I had gone downtown to the Acme Theatre with a friend to see *Davy Crockett*. We were sitting in the movie theater, eating popcorn and having a good time. Then the usher comes down the aisle during the movie with a flashlight, and when he got to my aisle, he shined his light on me. My cousin Jim was with him, and he said, "Come on, Gayle. We got to go. Your dad's been hurt real bad," and they hurried me out of the theater.

Jim's car was parked right by the front door. I got in, and we started racing. The wheels were squeaking. We were going through lights and all kinds of stuff—I'd never been on such a ride before. Then we rolled up to the hospital and they left the car running right in the street and we ran inside.

There was a whole bunch of people in the hospital, and they were talking about Dad and about his accident, but I couldn't follow it. I didn't know what they were talking about.

Pretty soon, Mom said, "Well, he might as well go home and get some rest," so Jim took me home, dropped me off. I went to bed, and when I woke up I could hear people talking again. Mother opened the door to my bedroom, and she just kind of stuck her head in and said, "He's gone." She was crying. Then she left. And that was it. Dad was gone.

Sheryl: What was it like there in Riverton after he died?

Gayle: Riverton was full of people who knew about me, who knew about the accident, who knew about the kid who had lost his dad in the oil field. People were nice to me all over the place.

But after the accident, I was lost. It seemed like I was all by myself. Mom got married within the year to a soldier who had returned from the war—a hero, but he wasn't my dad. Then, Mom died two years later, and I was an orphan. My only hope was to do as Dad always said, which was "Give it your best shot, and never give up."

So I graduated from high school in Riverton and wanted to go to college like Mom and Dad had talked about. And so I went up to Northwest Community College. It was in Powell, where a lot of the oil field work took place.

I was scared to death that I was going to lose all of my memories of my father, and that pretty soon he would be out of my life, because you forget things. And so I knew if he was going to be in my life—if I was going to be able to tell my children what my dad was like—I needed to work very hard at remembering. And when I met you, Sheryl, I started telling you about my dad and my mom, and my whole life. And at eighteen we eloped. I was so desperate for a family after I didn't have one anymore. And then we didn't wait long to get started on a family, did we, Sher?

Sheryl: Yeah, but then we were starving, and so you went back to the oil fields.

Gayle: Yep, I had a lot of relatives in the oil field, and I could break out roughnecking, which is the low man on the totem pole on a drilling rig. The rig I worked on had two men die on it a couple of months before I started. But I didn't worry about the danger. I was just thinking about getting home to my family. And so we made some money, and I went back to college, and eventually graduated. And then I got my doctorate from the University of Wyoming. But I still have the picture of that first rig I worked on. It saved us.

Sheryl: What do you think your dad would say about your life?

Gayle: Oh, I think he'd be proud. Dad was thirty-four when he died. I'm almost seventy-three right now. And I'd like him to know that I've lived my life thinking of him, always.

Always, always, forever. And maybe, when we get to heaven, he will be there. I'd like to give him a hug, smell his pipe to-bacco, and have a laugh. I'd like to tell him some of his stories and see if he agrees that's exactly how it was. I think it was. That's what I really believe.

RECORDED IN CHEYENNE, WYOMING,
ON MARCH 21, 2015.

| III |

HEALERS

ONCOLOGY NURSE
DANA VIVIANO, 37, TALKS
WITH HER DAUGHTER,
SARAFINA VIVIANO, 10.

Dana Viviano: Fifteen years ago, my mom got very sick. We took her to many doctors, and no one could figure out what was wrong. Then we transferred her to a cancer center, and the physician told us that she had stage-four cancer and that they didn't expect her to survive. It was very frightening.

Sarafina Viviano: So is that why you wanted to become a cancer nurse?

Dana: Well, I know it changed what I wanted to be when I grew up. I had always thought I wanted to be an ICU nurse; I wanted to jump out of helicopters at car crashes and pick people up off the field. But I watched your grandmother, and I remember thinking that there was a way they could have told us that she had cancer that was different. It was very cold, the way it was said to us at that time, and I remember being very angry. They didn't offer us any treatment; we were just supposed to take her home and let her die. We didn't really know what to do.

For the first month of her diagnosis, she was in the cancer center where I was training for nursing school, and so it was easy for me to come visit her. The nurses knew me, and they would let me come at night after visiting hours, when it was quiet. I'd sit in her recliner and she would sit in her bed and we would talk. I got to know her not as my mom but as a person, and we just had very frank and honest conversations.

Growing up, my relationship with her was rough. She was very strict: I had to keep straight As, and she wouldn't let me date or wear makeup. So we fought a lot. And it was hard, because just when I thought we were connecting again, I started to lose her.

Because she knew she wouldn't be here to see me graduate, she made me promise that I would finish my nursing degree, and that I wouldn't take time off of school to grieve for her. I think she knew if I stopped I might not finish, and I think she was right. She died October 11, during my midterms.

Sarafina: When your mom died, did that make you push yourself further?

Dana: I think so. I remember allowing myself to be sad at the funeral, allowing myself to be sad afterward. I didn't get out of bed that much, and I hardly ate. And then all of a sudden this sweet little voice said to me, *You need to finish. That's what you're meant to do.* And I did. I went back to class, and somehow I made it to graduation. And all along the way I think she's always been there to push me.

Two years after I graduated from nursing school, I took a job at Cardinal Glennon Children's Hospital on the cancer floor—and I can't imagine doing anything else. I love seeing these patients, and having the privilege to know a piece of their life. I laugh with them; I cry with them. I honestly can say I enjoy coming to work every day.

When you go in my office there are pictures of my patients, and a lot of them have passed now. I miss them when they're gone. They all teach you something. I learn about fear and I learn about hope. And I really learn that it's OK to let a person go.

Working here and doing what I do, I miss my mom, but maybe I can give people something my mom didn't have: some laughter, a hug. Even if I can't cure patients' cancer while they're here, maybe I can provide them peace.

Sarafina: I really think God wanted you to be what you are, because you're awesome at it. To me, you are maybe an angel on earth; you come down and try your best to heal people.

And you make patients smile, I can see. It's truly amazing what you do. You're my hero.

RECORDED IN CREVE COEUR, MISSOURI, ON APRIL 24, 2009.

HOSPICE CHAPLAIN
ISSAN KOYAMA, 60, TALKS TO
HIS SPOUSE, PAUL BOOS, 57.

Issan Koyama: When I was a teenager, my father was sick with cancer. One day my mother came to me and said, "I need a break. Can you sit with him?" I said, "Sure." I didn't know anything about taking care of anybody.

I was all alone with my father. At that time in Japan, parents didn't really touch kids, particularly boys—fathers and sons didn't touch. But he started to move his arm toward me. He was actually holding his hand out to touch me.

I held his hand, and eventually I held him in my arms. Hand to hand, chest to chest, head to head. He looked at me and took three separate exhales, with long pauses in between—his final breaths. I was really calm when he died. It's a strange thing to say, but it was so beautiful that I completely forgot to press the bell to ask for help. I really wanted to hold on to that moment.

The town I was raised in is a beach town—you're constantly looking at the ocean, and you start to wonder, *What's in it?* As a child, I wanted to become a scuba diver and explore the bottom. At one point I also was attracted to the idea of becoming a fireman—getting inside the fire, going right to the center of it. Going toward something unknown has always been what I wanted to do.

Paul Boos: So, what brought you to leave Japan?

Issan: Right after I graduated from college, I got a job in Paris at a fashion-industry newspaper, reviewing fashion collections.

In 1981, during a very cold winter, I used to go down to the Tuileries Garden and read this GLBT magazine called *The Advocate*, because I was really craving to read something in English. One Sunday in January, an article caught my eye about a "mysterious gay cancer." That was the first day I ever read anything about AIDS and HIV.

By the time I was transferred to New York in 1983, it was the beginning of the AIDS epidemic. Every day I dealt with people in fashion, art, theater, entertainment—and those communities were hit by AIDS most profoundly early on, and so I found myself in the epicenter of the epidemic. Particularly in fashion, everybody's so beautifully dressed and cared for. Suddenly, in front of you, all these beautiful men and women start to shrivel up and die.

It was a surreal time, going to all these funerals of my

friends and business colleagues. And there were lots of suicides. At that time many people chose to kill themselves rather than go through the final stage of the disease, which is so humiliating and deforming. Two of my friends hung themselves. And I started to feel, *I must do something.*

I wanted to go right to the center of it, to know better. And so I began to volunteer in the AIDS ward of a hospital. On my first assignment, I was called in because there was a Japanese-speaking patient who couldn't really put English words together. This young doctor told me, "This guy has AIDS, and he's going to die. You go into the room and talk to the mother and tell her to take the son back to Japan as soon as possible to have him die there. That's your job."

I go to his room in the isolation unit. The door was closed, and on it there was a long list saying, "You have to wear this gown; you have to wear these scrubs." On the floor outside the door there were three trays of meals—breakfast, lunch, and dinner. No one was willing to go inside to bring him food.

I thought, *Should I glove myself? Should I put on a gown? No. I'm not going to catch anything.* And I opened the door. I don't remember what I said to him, but I do remember this skeleton-like figure trying to sit up in the bed to talk, and his mother crying.

I think that experience actually set the tone of my years to follow. I started to really study Buddhist meditation, because it brings you calmness. Then I heard about this man Issan—*Issan* means "sits like a mountain." Before he was Issan, he was a hippie, and I think he was a drug pusher, and a transvestite. And in the midst of this whole flower generation movement in San Francisco, he discovers Zen.

This meditation practice really transformed him, and he eventually gets ordained and was assigned to this little meditation center in Castro District. One day he sees somebody who's homeless and dying of AIDS, and he picks this guy up and brings him home. And the next day he brings another one— and another one comes, and another one. Eventually this meditation center becomes one of America's first AIDS-specific hospices.

So one day I decided to go to San Francisco and look for him. I really didn't have any information. I thought if I go to Castro District and ask around, I would probably find the place. I knocked on the door—and then knock, and knock, and knock, and I almost give up. But then suddenly someone opens the door. This is a white guy in traditional Buddhist clothes, and I thought that was Issan.

I think my grief was really built up at that point, and without me really realizing it, I just broke down. This guy gently ushers me into the living room, and he sits and patiently listens to me for a long time. He says, "I am so sorry you didn't know. Issan also died of AIDS. I take care of this place now." He said that morning a guy upstairs checked out, and if I wanted to, I could stay in that room and learn how to take care of the people who were dying of AIDS. I said yes.

That got me connected with Zen Hospice Project. It's a large group of Buddhist priests and monks, which eventually brought me back to New York to start hospice work professionally. Later on, when I became a Buddhist priest, someone who ordained me gave me the name Issan. But I'm a little Issan—I'm a small mountain in comparison to him.

One night I had to go to the hospice center because a patient was dying. She was in pain, so there was lots of anxiety going around among the family members who were at her bedside. Then everything calmed down, and she died toward the dawn.

By the time I was able to leave, it was around ten o'clock in the morning. I step into the street. Behind me, there's a lot of pain and suffering. But just outside the door, life is going on. Cars are honking; everybody is rushing, has places to go. It's just another normal day.

I look up, and it was this beautiful summer morning, with an incredibly blue sky. I had this very strange feeling—and then it dawned on me: despite all the difficulties, everything is in perfect harmony.

I feel the energy of those people who passed away. I had the wonderful privilege to get to know them, and be a part of their caregiving. We had very intimate conversations, the type that normally don't happen in daily life but sometimes you really crave. About love, about life, about death—things you kind of feel a little frightened by but we felt safe to talk about. We created an immense sense of connection by sharing those really

intimate thoughts. And I really feel supported by the legacy of their lives. It keeps you going.

RECORDED IN NEW YORK, NEW YORK, ON JULY 17, 2015.

Paul Boos (*left*) and Issan Koyama.

RETIRED FIREFIGHTER
JOHN VIGIANO, 68, TALKS TO HIS
WIFE, JAN VIGIANO, 65,
ABOUT THEIR TWO SONS,
FIREFIGHTER JOHN VIGIANO JR. AND
POLICE DETECTIVE JOE VIGIANO,
BOTH OF WHOM DIED IN THE
SEPTEMBER 11 TERRORIST ATTACKS.

John Vigiano: Our son Joe loved the fire department. His birthday present was that he would come and spend the night in the firehouse where I worked. The guys I worked with would take a milk container and cut out the facsimile of a building, and they'd put it on the top of his birthday cake and light it up. Then Joe would throw a pot of water on it. The cake was a little soggy, but this is what he wanted!

He started dating a young lady whose father was a police

officer, and he came home one day and says, "I'm taking the police test." I says, "Joe, you're only seventeen years old." He says, "No big deal."

The day he took his police exam, we pull up in front of the school and I'm watching the candidates. Most of them were men, college-aged or older, and here's this baby-faced seventeen-year-old going in there. I said, "It's going to be kind of tough, but don't worry about it—you fail it, you fail it. We're going to go to the diner, and I'll come by here in about an hour and a half."

So we went to the diner, and within an hour he walks in: "That test was a breeze. Piece of cake." I said, "When are they going to give you the answers?" He says, "Tonight." About ten thirty that night he called me up from his girlfriend's house. I said, "What'd you get?" He said, "I aced it."

They assigned Joe to East New York, where I started my career. The first night he was working, I was also working, and I see him standing underneath one of the awnings.

So we stopped the truck, and all the guys got out. They wanted to rag on him because this was the kid that had his birthday party in the firehouse every year. He comes over and he kissed me, and he shook hands with and kissed the firemen that were closest to me. I said, "How do you feel?" "Fine. No big deal." I remember looking in the mirror, seeing this kid. Nothing was a big deal for him.

Our other son, John, wanted nothing to do with police or

emergency service or fire department. He wanted to be the next Donald Trump. He was going to make a million dollars and take care of his mother and father.

But in 1984, I came down with throat cancer. He noticed then how my unit took care of us. Every day, one of the men picked up my wife and brought her to the hospital where I was. This impressed John, and he says, "I'm going to become a fireman." I says, "You're kidding me. Firemen don't make millions of dollars. How am I going to live like a king?" *[Laughs.]*

But I was very happy, very proud. My father had been in the fire department, and he was the first one to be issued badge number 3436. When I came on the job, my father was still on the job, so obviously I couldn't get his badge. But when John decided he wanted to be a firefighter, they reissued it to John.

Both the boys would call me before they were working. John would always call around three thirty, four o'clock. That particular day, September 10, we spoke for a few minutes. And I says, "Be careful. I love you."

And he says, "OK, I'll be careful. I love you."

Joe called me around ten to eight the next morning, and told me to turn on the television, that a plane just hit the World Trade Center. I said, "I have the radio on, and nobody knows what kind of plane. What is it, small?" He said, "I don't think so, Dad. There's a lot of smoke. I'm heading south on West Street. This is a big one."

And I just says, "Be careful. I love you."

He said, "I love you, too." That was it.

We had Joe for thirty-four years, John for thirty-six years. Ironically, badge number 3436.

I don't have any could've, should've, or would'ves. I wouldn't change anything. There's not many people I know of that the last words they said to their son or daughter were "I

love you" and the last words they heard were "I love you." So that makes me sleep at night.

RECORDED IN BALDWIN, NEW YORK, ON MARCH 22, 2007.

IRONWORKER KERRY DAVIS, 52, TALKS WITH HIS COWORKER AND FRIEND KEN HOPPER, 53.

Kerry Davis: We've worked together as ironworkers on the Golden Gate Bridge for twenty-five years. It's a unique job, because there's only a few of us out there. We maintain the actual structure of the bridge, climbing in places where nobody else really goes. We like to say that we do everything "high, heavy, and hard"; we do all the stuff that nobody else wants to do.

Ken Hopper: But it's awesome—we get paid to climb around on the world's biggest jungle gym.

Kerry: We have to be 100 percent safe when we do our thing, because we can't really afford any mistakes. We have no protection for the tourists walking on the sidewalks below us. We drop something and it becomes newsworthy. We don't want that, so we take our time.

As we're working, we check in with each other: "Do you have this? Can I move this now?" We give things back and forth to each other. We've worked together for so long, we finish each other's steps.

Ken: Yeah, after we'd been working together for a while, people literally started calling you Ken, and they'd call me Kerry, because we were together so much.

When we go up we have to wear a full-body harness, and we are tied off at all times. When you start walking up the bridge, it's pretty flat at first, then it'll start angling up, and pretty soon it's kind of steep. You're hanging on to this cable wire, and the steeper it gets, the tighter you hang on.

Kerry: And you go up to the very top of the tower—about five hundred feet. People don't know that that's one of the coldest places on Earth when the wind blows and the fog comes in.

Ken: But being able to go out there and work on the bridge, every so often I have to stop and be a tourist and just look— even to this day—because I see it from a different angle. It'll be a really clear day, and I'll just never have really seen the bridge in that aspect.

Kerry: Right, I do the same thing. The bridge is our corner office, and you just have to stop and take it all in.

I like the freedom of our job: we go out, and there's nobody there to bother you or pressure you. And nobody can hear what we're doing but us.

But I guess at some point we ought to talk about one of the hardest things we have to deal with. . . . People will come out to end their lives. And we see that. It's tough.

Ken: You get to where you can recognize indicators: if they've been in one spot for a long time, if they're out there and it's really cold and they don't have a coat. Or they're by themselves, not really doing the tourist thing and looking at the view. Even crying—that's really a good indicator.

I've gotten to the point where I'll walk up to them, and after a while I'll just flat out say, "Are you thinking about jumping off this bridge today?" And a lot of times that actually gets a reaction where they're shocked that I'm asking, and I've had them truly answer, "Yeah." And then we have to do what we can to get them off the bridge.

Kerry: I had one instance where a guy started talking to me. He was a bartender in San Francisco, and he couldn't find a job. I asked him if I could climb over and talk to him, and he let me get within his space. He was on one side of the suspender cable, and I was on the other side. I grabbed the cable, reached around, and I just latched on to him. And I says, "Man, you know, things may look bad now, but it'll get better." And he actually said thank you—he didn't know what he really wanted to do.

Another time I went out after a girl that looked like she's about the same age as my daughter. She had taken her keys, her shoes, and her socks and had thrown them in the water. She was lying there on the cord, and my coworker climbed over to her, and I was right there. And as soon as he got close enough to grab her, I jumped over the rail and I grabbed her, too.

It's really hard to see somebody who's that low. Usually we talk amongst ourselves, we kind of debrief along the way: what went right, what went wrong. And you know, that's when we actually let things out.

Ken: There's hardly ever any closure. I mean, you know, we're worried: *Well, what happened to this guy? Is he OK?* There's a lot of unanswered questions.

Kerry: Yeah, and there's a feeling of elation when you finally *do* connect with them in some way. I'd say we've rescued 90 percent of the people that we've gone out after.

Ken: Some have even called us Guardians of the Gate, and that's nice to hear. It feels good.

Kerry: Well, I just want to say that working on the Golden Gate Bridge has been a lifetime achievement; I really do appreciate the time that I've spent there. And to meet people like you, and all the rest of the people that I've been working with—it's more than just a coworker thing; it's been an honor.

RECORDED IN SAN FRANCISCO, CALIFORNIA, ON JUNE 13, 2009.

Kerry Davis *(left)* and Ken Hopper.

SANITATION WORKER
ANGELO BRUNO, 60, TALKS
WITH HIS FORMER PARTNER
EDDIE NIEVES, 55.

Angelo Bruno: You have to work in sync when you're picking up the garbage: bend together, lift together. There's some days you and your partner are doing fourteen hours together—more time than with your wife or your girlfriend at home. It's like a marriage.

My old partner had retired, and you seemed like the kind of guy I could work with. So I went over to you one day, and I told you, "Eddie, I'm looking for a new partner. I know I can be a little difficult, because I do have some set ways, but give me a try." You were graceful enough to say, "Sure, why not?" And we hit it off from the beginning.

Eddie Nieves: We might have had maybe one disagreement in

seven years. We used to try to have the same day off, so we'd know: *I work with him, he'll work with me.*

And I learned a lot from you. I learned how to eat good on the route, because I used to eat pretty bad. I would eat anything—burgers, fried chicken, chicken wings—

Angelo: That doesn't go with me.

Eddie: [Laughs.] With you, I had to start eating bran muffins, whole-wheat bread.

And I learned a lot from you about how to talk to people. Everybody would come out just to talk to you.

Angelo: People would say, "Oh, good morning, Angelo! Good morning, Eddie! You want a cup of coffee? You want lunch?" Somebody would run and get us a scarf to cover our neck if it was cold out.

Eddie: He knows everybody on the route. They know what time it is when you come down the block. If you do the route different, they're going to say, "What happened?" This one lady, she's around seventy-five years old, and she really don't have nobody to talk to. So when we came on the block, she would be waiting for Angelo, because he would talk to her.

And the kids, when they hear the truck coming down the block, they'll be running to the window: "Angelo, Angelo!" And Christmastime, you would get 'em a gift; Halloween, you would bring them candy.

We had nuns on our route, too, and they kept kissing us—I never had that before!

Angelo: [Laughs.] The younger guys would ask me, "How did you get that?" It's just a little "Good morning," "Have a nice weekend," "Hey, you look great today." It's easy to be nice.

Or if we saw one of the ladies with a carriage, and they had to get the baby down the steps—what, I can do fourteen tons of garbage, but I can't lift a baby carriage off a step and carry it down? Or hold someone's baby when they went to get their car? The garbage ain't going nowhere. When you get it, you get it. I didn't look at it as going down the block to pick up garbage. I was going down the block to see my friends.

I'm a Vietnam veteran, I did two tours in the jungle . . . and I came home from that. So I don't pass the flowers up; I smell them. A lot of guys used to try to rush to get done, and maybe get back to the garage and hang out a little bit. And that's OK. Everybody has their own way. But I always like the street; I always like talking to the people.

Eddie: I used to come on the route and just look straight—come to work, pick up the garbage. But now when I go down the block, I look to see who's there.

Angelo: When I first came on the job, there was one old-timer, Gordy Floch. Six-four, solid hands. One day, he stopped the truck and he tells me, "Angelo, look down this block. See all this garbage? Sidewalks all crowded up?" I didn't think nothing of it. My father always told me to respect my elders.

So it took us about forty-five minutes to finish the block, and he stops me again. "Get out of the truck. Look back. Nice and clean, right? People could walk on the sidewalk. Baby carriages could go through. Guys could make deliveries. Be proud of yourself. You did that."

Eddie: The day that people learned that you were going to retire, we went maybe a block or two blocks, and six people came up to you and said, "Why are you retiring? You're crazy! What am I going to do when you leave?"

Angelo: I never thought my last day would be so emotional for me. I'm a little bit of a marshmallow anyway, but this—it really broke me up.

You know, if I had to pick a career all over again, I wouldn't pick no different. I miss the route terribly—I'm like that little kid looking out the window now when I hear the truck. But everybody should have a career like I had, and walk off the

job the way I walked on it. I think I could've done another thirty-one years.

RECORDED IN NEW YORK, NEW YORK, ON JULY 24, 2010.

Angelo Bruno *(left)* and Eddie Nieves.

VETERANS CRISIS HOTLINE WORKER RICH BARHAM, 57, TALKS WITH HIS COLLEAGUE NELSON PECK, 65.

Rich Barham: I have over twenty years of military service. I've been deployed eight times: I was in Vietnam, I was in Grenada, on Desert One getting hostages out of Iran, and I did some stints pulling security as a military police officer in Honduras, El Salvador, and Nicaragua. I was in Afghanistan, where I was in charge of mental health in a prison, and then I was stationed in Iraq, in charge of moving all the wounded.

When you're in a war zone, it's high speed and no sleep—and you're focused on it the whole time. And so I remember when I came home from Iraq, it felt like I walked into a brick wall. Everything just slowed down and stopped.

I actually sat in my backyard for about thirty days. I thought that I was just processing what happened to me, but after those thirty days my wife came out and said to me, "You need to talk to somebody." So I did. I was told that I had post-traumatic stress disorder from my years of deployment.

Nelson Peck: I had PTSD as well, and never realized how bad it was. I was a combat veteran with the United States Marines in Vietnam as a radio operator for an artillery unit. When I came back in the late sixties, I was taking Valium three times a day for a year and a half; it's a blessing that I'm still alive.

Suicide was a significant problem for Vietnam veterans. I saw so many die after Vietnam, and it was a real struggle for me to see that happen. So I wanted to make sure that I did something about it, and I got involved in developing the suicide hotline with the VA.

I'm responsible for training every single individual that comes through the hotline, regardless of the job that they do: the help techs, who are responsible for making sure that no veteran falls through the cracks, and the call responders, who take the calls from the veterans and work with them. And Rich, I know you take your job as a call responder very seriously. From day one you always excelled at talking to veterans who were in troubling situations, and you were able to bring them back.

Rich: It was easy for me to connect with the veterans, because I really understood where they were coming from. I remember on the first day, the first four phone calls we got were all rescues, where someone was trying to hurt themselves. That night, I was feeling like, *OK, this is for real.*

Initially, we had a lot of Vietnam veterans, a lot of Korean War veterans, a lot of World War II veterans. And probably about six months into the hotline, we started to get a lot more Afghanistan and Iraq war vets. I remember one rescue that I was involved in. A young gentleman had called me while he was in the middle of a flashback, and he had boarded himself inside his living room. He believed at that time that he was in Iraq. He had three young children; they were sleeping upstairs. I heard something click in the background, and I asked him if he had a weapon, and he said he did. I remember talking with him, and he was really anxious and incoherent—and then I lost the phone call.

So I called back and I got the answering machine. And the voice that I heard on the machine was totally different from the voice that I had been talking with on the phone. And it gave me the sense that, *Here's what this guy sounds like when he's not having a flashback. I know he can be OK if I can get him back to this place.* And you know, we *were* able to get him some help, and make sure he and his children were safe. Some of this guy's experiences were similar to mine, and I remember after that phone call being a little jerky and nervous, going outside, smoking a couple of cigarettes, and then just coming back in and doing my job again.

Nelson: Our job is not only to listen to the veteran, but also to put ourselves in the environment they're in so we can understand and help them in any way we can. I still go to counseling, even now, once a month. I call them my tune-up sessions. It's just a time to go in and talk to someone to make sure I never get back to where I was. And in our work, we're helping vets get back to the point where they can be like that as well. I think every single person on the hotline feels that way. We each give something that helps bring something positive back to veterans.

Rich: Sometimes you get on the phone with these vets and even banter helps. You start throwing the slang around, whether I know you're a Marine and say *jarhead*, or in the Air Force and we say *flyboy*. And we start laughing about some of the stuff; it's kind of like being in a war zone again. You're getting bombed one minute, and then you're cracking up the next. I mean, I've had conversations with vets where I was laughing my head off. A lot of it has to do with just hearing what they have to say and reflecting back that you understand.

I'm Native American, and we have what we call "hollow bone medicine." And basically what that means is that I need to get rid of all of my stuff so I can be there for someone else. And so in doing that at the hotline, it's kind of like I've been there for me, too. When I came home from Iraq, I made a commitment to myself that I would never again take anything for granted, especially life. And every day that gets reinforced by what we do for veterans.

Nelson: The hotline, by far, is the most rewarding thing I've ever done in my life. After Vietnam, I had survivor guilt—I never understood why I survived. But being with the hotline has really given me the answer: I was meant to be here to do this, so other veterans could survive.

RECORDED IN CANANDAIGUA, NEW YORK,
ON SEPTEMBER 26, 2012.

Rich Barham *(left)* and Nelson Peck.

EMERGENCY MEDICAL TECHNICIAN ROWAN ALLEN, 51, TALKS WITH HIS FORMER PATIENT BRYAN LINDSAY, 29.

Rowan Allen: A call came in just before my shift ended. I was a brand-new medic, and my first reaction was, *Oh man, right before we get off?* And then the dispatcher comes back on and says, "Child struck."

Luckily, we were just a couple blocks away. We pulled up, and I remember seeing your little bicycle with the front wheel twisted up. I saw the van, then I saw you—and it was scary. You had massive injuries to your head and face.

I remember your mother asking me in the ambulance, "Is he going to be all right?" And I didn't want to tell her anything that would scare her or make her lose control. You had a big dent on your forehead, and so I played it down and said, "Oh, it's just a little bump on the head." But to this day, when I start thinking about the details of the accident, I get choked up.

You wouldn't remember this, but my partners and I would come to the hospital every chance we got to check on you. You had so many wires and tubes, and your head was always bandaged in rolls and rolls of gauze. We didn't know how you would turn out.

Bryan Lindsay: All I remember is me getting on the bike, and then I remember waking up in the hospital, crying because I was in pain. I had been in a coma for two weeks.

It was second grade, and it was hard to adjust. I remember crying to the doctor, saying, "I don't want to wear a helmet at school." He said, "Don't worry, all the ladies are going to love your helmet." *[Laughter.]* But it was the complete opposite. It was torture. Kids would call me "helmet head." I couldn't play football or dodgeball; I'd have to sit on the side and watch. I wanted to be normal, like the rest of the kids. But my mom would say, "You're a strong person. God brought you back for a reason."

Rowan: Quite a few years later, one day we brought a patient into the hospital, and I heard this lady's voice. I didn't know who it was, but it stopped me dead in my tracks, and the hair on the back of my neck stood up. So I backed up and looked into this room, and there was this little short nurse with her back to me. It was your mother!

When she turned around and saw me, she jumped up and ran, and there was the two of us, hugging up real tight, just bawling. And everybody is watching us—this nurse and this paramedic in the middle of the emergency room, crying. I mean, it was a scene! *[Laughter.]*

Bryan: My mom was actually the manager of a bank, but then she went back to school for nursing, because you inspired her.

Rowan: I was so shocked! You know, people go into nursing for a lot of different reasons. But something like that? I have a lot of respect for your mother for giving up what she gave up to go into nursing. If—God forbid—I get sick, she's the kind of nurse I would want taking care of me.

We reconnected, and I would follow up with her every so often and ask her about you, and she'd say, "Oh, Bryan's this, and Bryan's that. Bryan's got a girlfriend now!" *[Laughter.]* And then one day your mom told me, "Bryan is going to be graduating. And I want you to come as a surprise."

Bryan: She set me up! *[Laughter.]*

Rowan: And then you guys turned around and you got me back, right?

Bryan: Yeah, we surprised you on *your* graduation!

Rowan: As I was coming to the end of my twenty-five years in EMS, to continue would mean getting promoted to lieutenant and going up the ranks. But in all the years I've been there, I've never done that, because anything above paramedic does not involve patient care. It's administrative—and that's not what I love to do. I like the hands-on nitty-gritty of emergency medicine. But I'm older now; the patients are heavier. So I decided to go into nursing.

Bryan: Three weeks ago my mother called me and said, "Clear all your plans for Friday; Rowan's graduating. And make sure you dress up nice!" So I said, "Cool—I'll be there!"

Rowan: You know, I've had patients who I'll visit in the hospital, go back and see if they made it, but you never know beyond that. But it was just something special about your case. To develop this kind of bond, it's ... I can't put it into words. This is what makes me do what I do.

Bryan: And I thank you. I really, sincerely thank you. Without you, I wouldn't be here. You're in the family.

RECORDED IN NEW YORK, NEW YORK,
ON JUNE 25, 2013.

Bryan Lindsay *(left)* and Rowan Allen.

ICU NURSE MICHELLE ALORE, 43, TALKS TO HER DAUGHTER, JENNA ANDERSON, 16.

Michelle Alore: When I was in college, I wasn't quite sure what I wanted to do. But I had your older brother when I was fairly young, and I decided nursing was a career that would allow me to take care of my family.

But I've realized that the reasons I initially thought I'd go into nursing aren't the reasons that I really love it. I now work in the intensive care unit. For people who deal with critical illness, sometimes it seems like it's just another day. But for patients and families in the ICU, sometimes it's their last day. So we try to do what we can to make people feel better, to keep them out of pain, to help them deal with crisis, with tragedies, and with death. And sometimes getting better is a painful process, so we try to make each day a good day.

Jenna Anderson: Can you share a time when you really bonded with a patient and the family?

Michelle: There was one patient about your age who came into the ICU. Two or three days prior, she had been a completely normal, healthy teenager. But then she experienced really bad heart failure, and she needed a transplant. She was in our ICU for a few months, waiting, but as time went on she got worse and worse. And it became clear to us that she was never going to be able to have a heart transplant.

Her family never wanted to give up hope. They just had this incredible courage that gave us a lot of hope, too. But we just couldn't fix her, and we had nothing to offer other than keeping her out of pain and taking care of her family.

When we recognized that it was nearing the end, I felt like I had to do something. And I decided to make her family a patchwork quilt. So one day I asked her dad for some pictures of her. I wanted the quilt to be something that would fit her personality, so after work I went to the fabric store and picked out about ten different patterns, all bright and in pinks and purples, her favorite colors. Then I stayed up all night and I made her family this quilt, and at the center was a picture of her outside on a swing, with her long, dark, beautiful hair.

I brought the quilt with me the next morning, and all the nurses went down to her room with me. We presented her father with it, and he just broke down and cried. She died shortly after that, surrounded by her family, and by the nurses. And at the funeral, her parents had the quilt hanging there.

Jenna: How do you stay positive when a patient dies?

Michelle: I believe the most important time in families' lives is when a loved one dies—and I think it can be a really beautiful time, too. Families can actually feel good about it when they do it on their terms. So I have to do what I can as a nurse to make an environment where families feel like they said everything that they needed to say and did everything that they could do—because death is final. I want to make sure that families feel comfortable with the decisions that they make so that they don't have regrets about those last moments with their loved ones. And then I just hold their hand and bear witness to it; I don't necessarily need to say anything.

Working in intensive care, even when patients do leave the hospital, we don't always know what happens to them. We just had a young girl, nineteen years old, who we thought was not going to survive. She was in the ICU for probably nine months, and she was unconscious and having seizures the entire time. But just recently, she came back to visit us. And when she came in with her parents, the entire unit stopped. Everybody came to see her—the doctors even came down from other floors—because we just don't often get to see when patients do get well. And it makes it feel like everything that we do is worth it.

Jenna: How do you let go after a difficult day in the ICU and come home to be our mom?

Michelle: You have to realize that you can't change everything, and you can't fix everybody. You just do the best you can, and if you feel like you're doing your best every day, you're able to kind of walk away from it and know that you're going to hand it off to someone else who's going to take good care of those patients and their families. Then I can go home and do my other job: taking care of you and your brothers.

You know, your older brothers have struggled a little bit and changed their minds several times about what they want to do. I think at some level, they think they want to do what I want them to do, but I have told them, "You have to do what *you* want to do. This is the rest of your life—you have to pick something that you're passionate about." And I would say the same to you: pick something that moves you, something that you're proud of—something you can keep getting up for and doing the next day. Because it's not easy; it's work. But it's what I love. So I would hope that you find something that you love, too.

RECORDED IN PHOENIX, ARIZONA, ON FEBRUARY 20, 2013.

Michelle Alore *(left)* and Jenna Anderson.

STORYCORPS FOUNDER DAVE ISAY, 46, TALKS WITH HIS FRIEND AUSTIN CHEN, 51, AN OB-GYN.

Dave Isay: So, where were you born?

Austin Chen: In Taiwan. And I grew up in Ecuador. It's a typical Asian immigrant story. My parents, they were comfortable in Taiwan. My father was a sea captain. But the desire for all parents in Asia is to send children to the United States for education. Instead of coming to the United States, which is much more difficult, they decided to go to South America. That was an easier stepping-stone. So that's where we ended up.

Later on, I came to New York to go to college, and I finished in three years. I wanted to go to medical school, but at that time you could not be admitted without a green card. So I started working in menial jobs. And I think I did that deliberately, because I wanted to see how other people's lives were.

I got a job with a cleaning company as a housekeeper. And most of the people that I worked with there were immigrants. We'd be picked up at a certain place, and we would all get in a van. Then we'd get dropped off in groups at different addresses, and we would do the cleaning. It was terrible—I still remember that feeling of when you are on the other end. There are a lot of things that are unfair, your supervisors are very critical, and you feel that you cannot get out. It's this hopeless feeling.

I cleaned houses for about a year, and it really helped me. In the hospital now, I know where the orderlies are coming from, and I always treat them with respect. Because, typically, when you're a doctor, the cleaning crew is not visible. I always tell them, "You should not feel that you are just the slaves around the workplace. You are very, *very* good at what you do." Being able to feel that you are good at what you do, regardless of your profession—that's the most important thing.

Dave: Did you ever tell any of the orderlies that you used to work as a housekeeper?

Austin: Yes, I did. And a lot of times they're skeptical. But when they see the way I tie my garbage, they can tell, because there are certain ways that they do things in the housekeeping industry.

Dave: Was there a moment that you knew what you were going to do with the rest of your life?

Austin: The exact moment? I still remember. We landed in

Los Angeles when we came from Taiwan. Our family was furloughed: we didn't actually go into the country; we were just waiting in the airport to take another plane to go to South America. And our parents' friends met us there in the airport. We were facing where the airplanes were, and their daughter asked me, "What do you want to do?" And I remember her tone being a little bit condescending.

Her family immigrated to the United States much earlier, and there was this sort of feeling about the newer generation of immigrants—like you're naive and haven't thought about all the hardships you have to go through. And I recognized that in her tone. So I just said, "I want to be a doctor." When I was young, I read the biography of an accomplished German physician, and I was very impressed.

I still remember that she said to me, "Even if you have to give up everything?" And I said, "Yes." She was just trying to tell me that, being an immigrant, there's a lot of sacrifice. But I knew I was willing to go through that sacrifice. In my mind, I promised myself that regardless of anything that's in my way, I'm just going to get through it. Because I always wanted to be a doctor. As a child, I felt like that was the most meaningful thing you could do.

Dave: When did you realize that you were going to be an ob-gyn?

Austin: I actually think ob-gyn was more like a default position. I've always been very good with my hands—I'm very crafty—and so I thought I was probably heading toward some surgical field. But then I spoke to a woman who told me that it took her ten years to become a surgeon, and I just felt like I wanted to go out there and do what I wanted to do immediately.

So I decided, rather than go through the whole surgical training, which is nine years and then a fellowship, I would do OB-GYN, which is four years. And once I started, I realized, *This is for me.* I knew in my heart, in my soul, that I'd be so much happier. I'll have contact with patients, and know their whole family, know their histories. And so OB-GYN turned out to be very good for me.

About twelve years ago, I started a solo practice. And before I actually threw myself into it, I thought about how my lifestyle will be. I decided that I would deliver all of my patients' babies. And I was totally prepared and mentally ready to do that.

Dave: So how many hours a week do you work?

Austin: I don't actually count those hours. I wake up, I work, and I go to sleep when I can no longer work. So that's what I do.

Dave: And you've worked seven days a week for the last twelve years without a single day off?

Austin: Uh-huh.

Dave: Wow, that's unbelievable. The sacrifices you've made . . .

Austin: Well, first of all, I don't think it's unbelievable. I knew exactly what I was doing. So this is not something like, "I am a martyr for the last twelve years." Definitely not. And you know, yes, there's a trade-off, but I wouldn't say sacrifice; sacrifice is like you do it for nothing. I feel like I get a lot of things in return. I am there for all my patients. And it's not just a promise; I really feel strongly about it. And that is the pleasure for me. I can make sure that their care is the kind of care that I would want for myself. I do not regret it at all. I just feel like I'm in disbelief that I made it.

But I would say, if there's *any* regret, it was that … I just want to compose myself a little bit. . . . My father died in 2000. I went to be with him, but I had a patient who was in early labor so I came back to New York. And when my father passed away, I was not there with him. . . . So that was the only thing. Yeah, that was it. *[Crying.]* Sorry, I didn't intend to cry.

Dave: Well, when you said to me that you wished, in your life, you had done something important enough that you could be on *Colbert*, I said to you that if you took 99 percent of the guests who have ever been on the show and you put them all together, they wouldn't hold a candle to what you've done.

Austin: Oh, I don't believe that. *[Laughs.]*

Dave: Well, I believe it's true. And I just want to thank you—on behalf of all the thousands of patients you've had, and all the babies that you've delivered—for being such an incredible doctor and such an incredible human being.

Is there anything you want to say to the children who you delivered who might listen to this one day?

Austin: Absolutely. I want them to unshackle themselves and do something that makes them *feel* good—even if it doesn't necessarily make everybody else feel good.

Dave: You're my hero, Dr. Chen. Thank you for everything.

RECORDED IN NEW YORK, NEW YORK, ON DECEMBER 8, 2011.

LILLIE COTLON, 70,
TALKS WITH HER SON AND
BUSINESS PARTNER,
BURNELL COTLON, 47,
A GROCER.

Lillie Cotlon: You were a very curious child from day one, and you were always willing to jump off into things you had no business doing. *[Laughter.]* I used to wonder why you would always leave home earlier than everybody else. I didn't know where you were going. But from what I understand, you were buying candy from a candy factory down the street and selling it at school. So that told me that you were an entrepreneur-type person.

Burnell Cotlon: Well, I learned a lot from you about how to prepare myself for the future. You and Paw Paw—your father—taught me *so* much about saving money, and about life. That's why when Katrina hit, I knew we were going to make it.

Lillie: A couple of days after we left the city for the hurricane, we're sitting in a shelter watching the TV, and it seemed like every levee in the city had broken apart. To sit there and watch the water *pour* into the city, and knowing nothing can stop it—my heart just flipped. We lost everything in Katrina. Everything.

Burnell: The city was on lockdown then. They was talking about how the ground was contaminated in the Lower Ninth Ward and nobody could ever move back, but I snuck back in because I was determined to see my home. When I finally got down there, I saw my house. It had floated from the foundation into the street; only a telephone pole stopped it from actually collapsing. Seeing my house floating like that, that's when it really hit me. It was the first time I cried.

I lived in a FEMA trailer in New Orleans for almost three years, and I stayed in that little box saving up every dime until I was finally able to rebuild my house.

But as I drove around the Ninth Ward, I saw we didn't have any shops. You have to catch three buses just to get to a store— and the closest one is a Walmart in the next city. I was taught if there's a problem, there's always an answer; somebody got to make a move.

Lillie: After Katrina you had been working in management at Burger King, at McDonald's, Family Dollar. I used to bring your lunch to you, and this one particular day when I saw you, I said, "Son, let me tell you something. I think you're in the wrong business. I suggest you sit down and think about what your next step in life is gonna be." I say, "Maybe it's some type of business of your own."

Burnell: You told me to get back to the entrepreneurial spirit that was already inside of me. And I'm glad I listened. I decided to open up a grocery store.

I remember when I first bought the building. It used to be a barbershop, but at the time it was full of trash. Everybody thought that I was crazy. I kept hearing, you know, "It's gonna take too much money. Nobody's gonna support you." It was a lot of negativity. But I didn't see it like that. I saw an opportunity.

Lillie: I remember when I peeked in the door before you started working, there was nails and debris on the floor that you had to crawl over. I said, "Oh, Lord, how can he make anything out of this?" The roof was badly damaged, too, and you were tearing it down—just you and your friend Walter. You was scaring the daylights out of me. I used to pray for you all the time: "Please, God, take care of these guys up here on this roof!" *[Laughter.]* But you got it done.

Burnell: Those eight-hour days easily start turning to fourteen-, fifteen-hour days, trying to finish. You know, it was real, real hard. But what motivated me the most was working up there and seeing the people with their groceries, coming from that Walmart. I'd see them get off the bus with all of those bags, and they would stop in the middle of the street just to relax, and then pick the bags back up and keep on going. And so we kept on going, too. Seeing that made me work harder.

Lillie: At the grand opening, the whole city hall was there. And I served the very first sno-ball.

Burnell: I will never forget that day. The first customer was an elderly lady. And I remember she cried because she said she never thought the Lower Ninth Ward was coming back.

Seeing all the kids and everyone out there, that's when it hit me that this dream I had of turning that shell of a building into a store was for real—and it really meant something.

Lillie: The Lower Ninth Ward was devastated. I mean, worse than any part of the entire city. But you had vision enough to see that this is a place that can be developed—you saw something that we didn't.

Burnell: It feels good, knowing that we made a difference in the community. After Katrina, we all was in the same boat. Everybody lost. But look at us today. We have the first grocery store in the Lower Ninth Ward—the first and *only* grocery store. And I'ma keep on going.

Just seeing so many people walk back and forth to the store, it's a joy—let alone drive to the store. I looked in the rearview mirror when we was leaving out today and saw two cars driving up. If they have a car, that means they *choose* to come here. That means we're doing something right.

All the headaches—all those hours rebuilding, hanging off the roof—was worth it for the look on my customers' faces when they walk through the door. And if it takes me do it by

myself, I'ma put one business at a time back into the Lower Ninth Ward. 'Cause it's home.

RECORDED IN NEW ORLEANS, LOUISIANA, ON APRIL 3, 2015.

ASSISTANT FEDERAL PUBLIC DEFENDER VITO DE LA CRUZ, 51, TALKS TO HIS WIFE, MARIA ANASTASIA SEFCHICK-DEL PASO, 47.

Vito de la Cruz: My mother and my father were not together when I was born. He was married to someone else, and when I was born my mother dropped me off with a neighborhood friend and left a note with my father's number on it. So my father picked me up and left me with my nineteen-year-old aunt, Iris de la Cruz, who I've always called Nena. Nena had just graduated high school when I showed up on her doorstep, but she embraced parenthood—and she didn't have to. She was wonderful. Even though I didn't meet my father until I was fourteen, my nena told me where I came from and who my father was, and had pictures of him in the house.

Our family—my aunt and uncles and my grandmother—

we used to travel from the barrio in San Benito, Texas, up to North Dakota and do the migrant farmworkers' circuit in the summers. We relied on the money that we would make during the summer migration to live off of for the rest of the year. And then Nena would also work part-time, and her income supplemented whatever the family earned on the migrant trail.

Maria Anastasia Sefchick-Del Paso: What was it like being a migrant farmworker?

Vito: Well, it was exciting because we were always going somewhere new. We passed through all these different states, crossing rivers and prairies and mountains. It was an adventure—all the family together, working side by side. On the weekends, we would make *barbacoa* in this pit in the ground out at these migrant camps, and Sunday mornings we would open up the pit and drag out the *barbacoa* and eat together.

But it was also equal parts hardship and poverty. I remember when I was thirteen or fourteen, there was an immigration raid in the tomato field where my family was working. Many of the crews were citizens, like we were, or resident aliens, but some were undocumented aliens coming across the border to work. This caravan of about six or seven green vans just stormed into the field, and people started stampeding. To this day I can smell the dirt and the fear. I could hear the noise the batons made as the border patrol beat them over the heads and on their bodies. And when I was about ready to turn and run, my uncle grabbed my shoulder and said, "Stay still." And I remember they just passed us by. They were chasing people who would run.

The good thing about my family is we stuck together. And when we were confronted with the raid that day, the family made sure that we stayed close. Some of them—to this day—talk about how afraid they were. I mean, people were being herded into a ditch, and then they were beaten and handcuffed and dragged away. It's been thirty-eight years, but it's still vivid in my memory.

I didn't know exactly *at that moment* that I wanted to go into law, but I saw people being afraid of other people with authority. It struck a profound chord in my being, because that's not the way we should be.

If there's one thing that my nena gave me, it was a desire to learn and to succeed in school. Against all odds, she was the first in our family—of either gender—to graduate from high school and eventually from college. And I ended up going from San Benito, Texas, to Yale, which was a culture shock to the extreme. I went from an environment where we were essentially surviving below the poverty line, to where our entire family could probably have existed for a month on all the food that was thrown away in just one dining hall at Yale. But I graduated in 1981, and then I went on to law school at the University of California, Berkeley.

After law school, I wanted to go back to where I started. So I started out working as a staff attorney focusing on employment issues, migrant housing, and migrant farmworker law. And now I'm a public defender in the Reno federal court.

Maria: Well, I think your family is very proud of you. I can tell in Nena's voice.

Vito: Thank you. The work is really an ongoing struggle. You know, there is a role for law enforcement—laws should be enforced; folks who violate them should be apprehended and prosecuted—but there is a dignity that sometimes gets forgotten, a human dignity that gets trampled on. And if we forget

that, we forget our own humanity. And so, if the things that I do while I live this life help improve somebody else's life, then for me, that's enough.

RECORDED IN RENO, NEVADA,
ON MAY 1, 2010.

POLICEWOMAN PAT HAYS, 74.

Pat Hays: When I was a kid, I was very, very shy. My dad used to come home drunk and just hit me. So I taught myself to read when I was four, because I was the quietest when I was reading and less likely to get hit that way. And so I read *a lot*—my whole life was the books that I read.

I left home at seventeen, and I married my high school sweetheart—well, my *sort-of* sweetheart. My mother loved him. Every time I wanted to break up with him and date other guys just to see if there were any interesting ones out there, my mother would lay on this guilt-trip: "Oh, he loves you so much." I went, "Oh, all right, Mom." I dropped out of high school to marry him, and I got pregnant within the month. So I went from my father's home to my husband's home, and I had my daughter ten months later.

My husband wasn't working, so I went out and got a job working the switchboard at a hospital. And when I brought home my check, he was like, "Give me the money!" I was like,

"It's my money; I earned it!" Unfortunately, he felt that it was OK for him to conclude arguments by hitting me, so, of course, he did. But I was not going to repeat my mother's life, and told him, "I'm not going to take this." I called the police, and that was it.

I worked the switchboard for a few more years. Then one day, when I was about twenty-four, my friend told me she was going to take the Chicago policewoman's exam. They were revamping the department, and as a consequence of that, they had formed a new unit for policewomen. And so I said, "Well, I'll go with you and take it, too."

Over a thousand women took that test, and from that, 219 names were posted—and we got the call to show up.

I just barely passed the physical requirements of height and weight. You had to be five foot three, and you had to be over 110 pounds. But I was only about five foot one; I had a crick in my neck the whole day from looking up to make conversation with people. I mean, these women were *huge*! But the guy who was measuring us just told me, "Stand on your toes." And he passed me. I had no experience whatsoever, and I never really wanted to be a policewoman, but I guess I'm stubborn. I was just like, "I'm going to finish this academy if it kills me!"

I was in the class of thirty-five women who came on the job in 1966. Our uniform was a navy skirt with a little box jacket and this ridiculous hat that was shaped like a sugar scoop. It didn't matter how many bobby pins you used; the damn hat would lift up in the wind and go trailing down the street. So you get a choice of losing your prisoner or losing your hat. Well, the hats were a one-of-a-kind deal—you couldn't find one to replace the hat that belonged to you. So of course we held on to the hat. We could always get the prisoner later. [Laughs.]

As policewomen, our duties were mostly in youth division: family investigations of abuse or neglect. Or, with a woman victim or offender, homicides and sex crimes. We would do on-the-street arrests of truants and school absentees and curfew violators. If they found a lost child, then they would call the women in, because the men really didn't want to deal with the children anyway.

I was assigned to what was believed to be the worst area, which was Maxwell Street. We would get runaways every day with allegations of neglect or abuse. And of course, when we found them, we would have to do a certain amount of counseling. That was an interest of mine, especially coming from a dysfunctional family. I wanted to be somebody who was warm and who you could sit and feel comfortable talking to.

You know, I was dressed for the role as an authority figure: you're wearing the uniform, you've got that big star on your chest, and you've got the gun on. And there's a certain power that comes along with that costume. But I also had to find a way to get past the star and the uniform and all of that, to communicate, "What can we do here?"

And so my background came in really handy, because I could say, "You know, I didn't just read this in a textbook. I lived it. I had a father like yours. So right now is the time when you should be saving your birthday money and your babysitting money, so that you'll be able to get out on your own." If I could do it, they could do it.

But there were a lot of situations where you don't know what to say. I had a rape victim once, and she really did not want to talk to anybody. But they knew I was good at talking to victims, so they called me. It was tough going. I felt so bad for her, and I wished there was something I could do.

And then I went to run my fingers through my hair, and as I did it, the shirt of my uniform ripped and my whole elbow popped out. And we just both started laughing. Then that turned into tears. And I just held her, and she cried, and she cried, and she cried.

A little bit of care and concern—that's about all you had to offer. Whatever they were confronting, the fact that you were willing to listen and try to offer them some comfort—even if it's saying, "I really admire the strength of character you need to be able to deal with this situation"—they felt better.

I bounced around to different assignments, and I was a detective twice—first in vice, then in the rape unit. And there was always this implicit, "You must be screwing *somebody* to get a good job like this." But that wasn't true. It never was true.

I didn't want my daughters to join the force, because I didn't want them to have to put up with the things that I did or see the things that I saw. And I *really* didn't want them to see the world from that point of view. You know, this job has got a really high divorce rate. By the time the thirty-five of us policewomen were on the job ten years, I would say that probably every single one of us had divorced. It's very hard on marriages, because saying "I'm going to put you in prison for ten years for rape," then going home and telling my husband "What would you like for dinner, dear?"—it just doesn't go well.

I retired in 2001, but in the thirty-four years I was on the force, it wasn't all adversity or I would have been really stupid to have kept that job. It's kind of a calling. I *really* enjoyed helping people. I would have done it forever.

I used to always work New Year's Eve, because I don't like New Year's Eve. My birthday's on January 2, so I get a year older and I lose a year all at the same time. Well, I was working it one year and I got a call, and this woman's voice said, "Miss Hays, you probably don't remember me, but you talked to me years ago, and I just wanted you to know that I straightened my life out. And I now have a two-year-old daughter, and I'm so glad that I talked to you." And I thought, *Boy, that's really God's blessing.* Because most cops are cops forever and nobody ever tells them things like that.

The police department is not big on telling you that you

did a job well. Your sergeants are not going to tell you how great you are—it's just not the nature of the job. So you have to be able to go home knowing you helped somebody along

the way, even if sometimes you can't change the outcome. It may not have been all that I would like for it to be, but I think I did some good.

RECORDED IN CHICAGO, ILLINOIS,
ON FEBRUARY 4, 2015.

INK REMOVAL SPECIALIST
DAWN MAESTAS, 42,
TALKS WITH HER CLIENT
NICOLE MENDOZA,* 22.

Dawn Maestas: I went to school for laser tattoo removal, and the moment that I put the laser in my hand, I had one of those aha moments that you hear about but you wonder if they'll ever happen to you. I just knew this was going to be my career. It felt so right.

One of the first tattoos that I removed was on myself. I'd had to look at my ex's name on my hand every day and know what he had done to me. This was a guy who locked his arms around my legs at night and made me ask for permission to use the bathroom, and who put a loaded shotgun to my head and told me all the reasons that he should kill me. So it wasn't just

---

* The participant's name has been changed.

a tattoo. It was like being in a car accident at an intersection: every time you pass that intersection, you remember the impact. And you live it over again every day.

When I finished laser school, I got in touch with a doctor and decided to start a tattoo removal office inside his clinic. And when you walked in my office, it was déjà vu. I saw me, all over again.

Nicole Mendoza: I was with a guy for five years who was really abusive toward me. When I finally tried to end it, he held me hostage and tattooed his name all over my body against my will. Afterward, I went into hiding with my family. One day they saw you on the news and wrote down your number about removing tattoos. That's when I called you.

Dawn: I knew what you were feeling inside. I knew the sickness, the loneliness, and the embarrassment all too well. And I was so angry that life had done to you what it had done to me. So when women come in under circumstances like ours, I remove their tattoos free of charge.

Nicole: The first time you removed one of my tattoos, I was just like, *Wow. I don't feel like a prisoner in my body anymore.* Each time you removed one, I felt like I was taking ownership of myself again. I wasn't his property anymore, and that felt really good.

Dawn: When we first met, you were so scared to make a decision by yourself. But the more time that we spent together as your tattoos were being removed, the more I got to see you coming to life. And now you're ready to show everybody how strong you are. I'm so proud of you and where you are today.

You know, I spent over half my life living in violence. And when I thought that I was at the point of losing my life, I used to tell God, "If You let me survive this, I won't leave anybody else behind. I promise."

So I feel very blessed to be able to make a living doing something I absolutely love to do. I went through some horrific situations in my life, but I realized that there was something beautiful that survived—something to build on. I get to help someone seal off one portion of their life and help them enter into the next.

Nicole: To be honest, it's still hard to grasp how you feel about me. I'm like, *Why would she care about me? I'm just a nobody.* But you remind me that I *am* somebody. And you took me under your wing, completely. It feels good to have someone who understands. I don't feel alone.

Dawn: That's all I could ask for.

RECORDED IN ALBUQUERQUE, NEW MEXICO, ON FEBRUARY 28, 2013.

FMF CORPSMAN
BARBARA BUTLER, 58.

Barbara Butler: I think it was the good Lord put me in the military, because He knew I was going to get in big trouble if I had stayed in New Jersey. *[Laughs.]* Back then, I partied hard, and I just knew I couldn't go through life partying all night. So I joined the Navy in 1977. I was twenty-eight years old.

Boot camp was extremely rough, being one of the oldest recruits there, so I had to work to hang in there with the younger ones. But I knew that I had to do my best or I would be out and back in Jersey where I started, and I did not want to go back.

During Corps School they asked for volunteers to attend extra medical training for Fleet Marine Force—FMF. And I looked around the classroom and nobody raised their hand, so I said I would volunteer. They got real upset and said, "It's for males only." But I said, "There's no gender prerequisite, so I want to go." There were six of us females in my class, and after I joined the rest of the girls said, "Well, we're going to go, too."

When we got to training at Camp Pendleton in California, they made it *extremely* hard for us. They'd make us run in front of the guys and just said derogatory things, like "Watch the bouncing cheeks!" But I never complained.

I told the girls, I said, "We're not going to cry in front of them." And so we cried and hugged each other within the confines of our barracks, and then we bit our tongues and gave it 110 percent when we were out there. These women were awesome. They wanted to make us quit, but we dug in our heels and we finished training. And it groomed us to be strong.

Later, when I reported for my first field assignment, they looked at me and said, "When did the females go FMF?!" I had eighty-five Marines that I was responsible for—and I was the only female out there.

One time, I told a Marine to be careful with a bowie knife, because it had a wicked blade. He said, "I've been doing this a long time—I got this." Well, within a few minutes I saw blood fly up in the air and I looked and he had severed some blood vessels in his hand. So when he passed out seeing his own blood, I used that as my anesthesia and I took a clamp and I reattached his tendons, sewed the vessels back, and dressed his hand—and then had them rush me to a medical facility so I could save it. When that Marine was able to move his hand again, no one said "good job" or "thank you," but the men did start calling me Doc. And I thought it was the most awesome thing I could have heard. That was enough for me.

When I got back from the field, I went on to school and became a surgical tech, then a surgical instructor and a field instructor. And I was able to do it because I started out as an FMF corpsman. I retired in 1998, and now I live just outside the back gate of Camp Lejeune.

We were the first women in the Navy to go FMF—and really, it was the best thing I could have done. It made me what I am today. I'm standing on the shoulders of Army women and Marine Corps women. And as I sit back as a retiree, it feels re-

ally good to know that we're leaving behind a legacy that will speak for us when we're no longer able to.

RECORDED AT CAMP LEJEUNE IN JACKSONVILLE, NORTH CAROLINA, ON MARCH 8, 2008.

ENGLISH TEACHER
AYODEJI OGUNNIYI, 24.

Ayodeji Ogunniyi: My father came to America in 1988 while my mother, my older brother, and I were still in Nigeria. Back home he was the manager of a big bank and he had a bachelor's degree, but none of those credentials could be used here in America, so he had to start from scratch. He boarded with a friend, got his chauffeur's license, and worked for about a year and a half as a cab driver until he made enough money to send for us in January of 1990. We were only supposed to come here for six months, but my mother said she wasn't leaving without him. So we decided just to stay.

I was three years old when we moved to Chicago's South Side. I remember being petrified at the snow. *[Laughs.]* I remember falling asleep at day care and waking up in the back of my father's cab. Some days, I wouldn't understand where I was, but I would just see the back of his head or hear the jazz radio station he loved, and I knew that I was with him.

For my parents, it was God, then education. My father worked to get my mother through nursing school, and she became the breadwinner. My mother always planned for everything—no matter what it was. She wanted to get us a home in the suburbs, so she worked long hours—some days sixteen hours. But she always prepared dinner and had things ready for us.

My father was more the free-loving, enjoy-every-moment-but-do-what-you-have-to-do type of person. I remember my father always sneaking in little things here and there, buying us toys that we had to hide from my mother. But he always made sure we had the homework done.

Our parents just wanted to make sure that my brother and I started right in America. So since I was a child, I was trained that I was going to be a doctor, and if not a doctor, an engineer. And if not an engineer, a lawyer. For the first fifteen years of my life, I thought that those were the only three occupations that were out there.

When I got to college, I was in the premed program, and I was going to be a doctor. I got straight As because the math and science came very natural to me, but I had no passion for it. I thought, *Do I really want to be a doctor?*

On Christmas break freshman year, I came back from school. It was December 22 and I was sitting at home in my room and it was just me and my father in the house. I walked into the kitchen as he was eating breakfast, and out of nowhere he started talking about how he met my mother. And then he told me about how my grandmother gave me my first name, Ayodeji. It means "sudden joy." Before he went off to work that day, he asked, "Is there anything you need?" And I said, "Just bring home some orange juice." He left and my friend called me and we went to the mall.

I came back home around 4:00 p.m., and I turned on the news. They said, "An unidentified male's body was found in an alley in Evergreen Park." Things like that on the news are so peripheral to us, I didn't think anything of it, and I just changed the channel. It was not until eleven that night that the knock came, and the police told us that man was my father and that he had been murdered. The next thing I remember is yelling "No!" really loud. And then my mother fell out, and I just had to hold her.

Within four days of the murder, the police solved the case. The murderers were eighteen, nineteen, and twenty-two. I was very, very angry. I didn't necessarily want to retaliate. I just wanted to ask them, *Why? What happens to a person? Where do they get lost and become murderers?*

At the time I was tutoring kids at an after-school program for some extra money, and these kids came from the same impoverished conditions as the people who murdered my father. One student in the program—he was probably around sixteen years old—always had this terrible attitude. We were doing something where everyone had to read out loud, and when it was his turn to read, he just stormed out of the classroom. I went out and I asked him, "What's going on?" and he just broke down. He said, "It's hard for me to read."

There are many people that cry because they're hurt, they've been neglected, but to cry because you couldn't read? So we got him in some other programs, and he started to read—it was just, like, this *gift* for him. And by me giving that to him, it was sort of like a healing mechanism for me. I forgot about the pain of the murder, and I wanted to continue to give more of what I had to these students.

I realized that everybody at some point sits in a classroom—*that* could be the foundation for everything else. And then it dawned on me: *You have to do what you love.* So that's when I said, *I'm going to follow my heart and become a teacher.*

In my classroom, I always have my students fill out a questionnaire—questions like, *What is your favorite candy? What is the favorite book you've ever read? Who's the most important person in your world?*—so that whenever I see a student having an is-sue or something, I can refer to the question sheet and see, *OK, I'll give him a Snickers tomorrow.* And they're just, "How did you know this was my favorite?!" They forget that they filled that out. And they have this feeling of, *Wow, someone's taking an interest in me.* You can't put a price on that. And it keeps me going.

I would want my father to know that the moment he stepped into any one of my classrooms, my students would instantly know him by the principles that they learned from me and that I learned from him. I don't need any memorabilia to honor my father's life. I don't need pictures—just what I instill in my students. That really gives me peace: to know that whatever happened to my father is not going to be in vain.

RECORDED IN CHICAGO, ILLINOIS,
ON FEBRUARY 25, 2011.

| IV |

PHILOSOPHERS

LEE BUONO, 40, A NEUROSURGEON, TALKS WITH HIS EIGHTH-GRADE SCIENCE TEACHER, AL SIEDLECKI, 65.

Lee Buono: I had a patient that came in with a benign tumor pushing on the left side of his brain, which is the speech area. He could get some words out, but they were almost unintelligible. It's almost like someone's sewn your mouth closed. So I'm talking to his wife, and we tried to lighten up the situation, and she started asking me about myself. She said, "How long have you known that you want to do neurosurgery?" And I said, "Since I was a kid. I had this great teacher, and he told me I could."

After the surgery, the guy gets his speech back—he was crying; his wife was crying, just excited and happy. And then he says, "Don't forget to thank your teacher. Make sure you let him know." And boy, that stuck in my head.

I was driving home that night, and I was thinking, *I've got to call Mr. Sie.* And I got one of those Sharpie markers, and I wrote it on the back of my hand so I would remember. And in the morning, I called you.

Al Siedlecki: I was teaching physics, and it was a tough chapter. We were having a test the next day, and the kids really needed help. So when the phone rang I said to the secretary, "Tell whoever it is they have to call back." I was just ready to get to the critical part of this lesson, and I didn't want to be interrupted. But she says to me, "No, he's adamant. He says he needs to talk to you right *now*!"

Lee: [Laughs.] I was afraid you wouldn't call back, or she wasn't going to give you the message.

Al: I picked the phone up and you go, "Hi, it's Lee Buono." I say, "Lee, what's going on, man? I haven't heard from you since you were in high school!" It had been probably twenty years. You said that you wanted to thank me. You thought of me, after all these years.

I said, "Of all the people in your entire career, you want to thank *me*?" And I started to cry. It was the same feeling I had when my kids were born. The students in my class got so quiet. They said, "Oh, we're sorry." And I said, "Why are you sorry?" "Somebody died, right?" I said, "No, no, these are tears of joy." And I had to excuse myself and put cold water on my eyes, like I tell the kids to do.

Lee: I didn't think you were going to have that response. I thought it was going to be, "Hey, Lee, thanks for calling. I appreciate it."

Al: You hit the jugular, man. I'll never forget it my whole life.

What do you remember about science in eighth grade that you think led you to be a neurosurgeon?

Lee: It was the best class I ever had. I'd come in and be excited. Not just for the fact that there's science, but because there's going to be fun—and intrigue! You know the way teachers are: they get up there, they give a lecture, blah, blah, blah. But then here's you, like, making these funny voices. It wasn't coming into class and just trying to put your head on the table and sleep.

Al: Well, there's a certain enthusiasm I think the teacher has to bring—it's infectious. Like I go in there and say, "All right, you're not going to believe this class today! I'm not lying to you; you're really not going to believe it!" I don't want to teach just what's in the textbook. I'd much rather do my own thing to get the lesson across.

But you were also enthusiastic. And you just loved a challenge. I mean, anything new, you were like, "Oh, I can do that!" Somebody gave you that tenacity, that determination, long before you got into my class. I remember the way you got jazzed when we dissected the frog. Other kids left around three o'clock, but you stayed after school to dissect the brain and spinal cord. Very difficult task. But you were so meticulous about each little manipulation. I'm watching you from afar: "Yo, Lee. How you doing?" "I'm getting there. I'm getting there." You were really deep in thought, and I didn't want to interrupt you too much.

Lee: You just patiently said, "Take your time."

Al: You got to the tail piece on the end of the spinal cord, and I knew that you knew that you had to slow down. Most kids, they'll give it a tug, and that little tail piece will pop off. But you used a number 10 scalpel blade to lift it out. The brain and spinal cord were all in one piece, and you could see all the cranial nerve junctions. The lobes were perfect. Even the olfactory lobe was perfect. *Impeccable* isn't a good enough word. And you go, "I think I have it." You were looking up at me with your little goggles on. I said, "Lee, you could probably be a neurosurgeon. You're that good."

Lee: That's like saying to a kid, "You could be president of the United States."

Al: You have a gift, and that day I wanted to make sure you knew I absolutely recognized it.

There are magic moments that happen in a classroom, like you with that frog, when all of a sudden a student realizes that they might be directed toward their passion. There's no doubt about it when it happens. They get these great big eyes, and they won't blink, for fear they might miss something. It's no longer an assignment. It's something that they want to learn.

Teachers don't realize that they have a lot of power to make that happen.

Just like any career, you're going to have highs and lows. And lately, Lee, I almost am afraid to say to some people that I'm a teacher. But I'm not now, because you called me. You're the fuel that keeps people like myself going. I'm a teacher. It's my passion. And I'm going to help as many people as I can, as long as I can, to find their passion, too. That's something that you gave me back. I'm so happy that I had you as a student.

Lee: Are you kidding me? You changed my life! Thank you for allowing me to be where I am. Encouragement and patience—that makes the difference. I'm your student. Forever.

RECORDED IN MEDFORD, NEW JERSEY, ON AUGUST 16, 2011.

Al Siedlecki (left) and Lee Buono.

ARTIST AND EDUCATOR
SOL ARAMENDI, IN HER FORTIES,
TALKS WITH HER STUDENT
CYNTIA GOMAR, 31.

Sol Aramendi: I moved to New York twelve years ago from Buenos Aires. It was January—the weather is difficult, no? I didn't have any of the proper clothing. And I went from having family and a lot of friends to a place where I knew very few people. It took me three years to adjust.

A friend had invited me to start a business, but the business didn't work out, so I had to do something to survive. One morning I went to see the sunrise, and I took a picture of it. That first light gave me a lot of hope, I think, and that's when I started going around taking pictures.

First, I felt this compulsion to photograph grass. In New York! It wasn't easy to find. And then I had a dream one night of when I was a kid and my grandmother used to take me to the countryside and she would stop in the wheat fields and I would walk in this wheat field like I was swimming. For me, it was the best part. And all these New York pictures of blurry grass—they looked, also, like a sea of grass or like swimming in the grass. It reminded myself of where I was coming from. I needed that connection.

Photography helped me arrive in New York: *I am living here, this is my life now, these are the places I go.* It helped me realize that I don't live anymore in Argentina. After that, things changed completely. I made new friends; I felt more comfortable.

I said, *Okay, since photography's helping me feel at home in the city, I'm going to teach photography—in Spanish—to people who are immigrants.* Most of the time, immigrants are kind of second-class citizens. We are not welcome in many spaces, or we feel like we are not. So I'm reclaiming spaces that we think are not for us.

Why did you come to my class?

Cyntia Gomar: I wasn't happy. I was working Monday through Friday at a factory. I was making, I think, five dollars an hour, and I sent money to my mother. And then on Saturday and Sunday I was visiting family—and that was it. I had arrived from Mexico when I was sixteen, but I couldn't believe that I was really living in New York. You see in the movies that New York's a big city, a great place, but we didn't go to the places that are in the movies. And it was hard for me to learn the language, so when we would go out, I felt scared. That was my life for years.

Then, when I got pregnant with my daughter, I stopped working—so I was a full-time mom all the time, until I found out about your class. My friend told me, "I found a flyer about a photography class, and it's in Spanish. If you want to go, let's go together."

Sol: So what were your first impressions of me?

Cyntia: I found you kind of intimidating at first. You said, "Don't think about your past. Think about what you're doing now and what you want to do. See the city that you live in. Find out about it. Explore it. *Live* in the place where you live. You can do it!"

But taking pictures changed everything. I feel good when I take pictures; I feel free. I discovered that I can take good pictures, and I can see the city.

Before, I was always afraid of talking in public with people looking at me. But when I take pictures, and everyone's like, "Oh, show me!" it's not hard anymore. For me, taking the class, it was freedom. I'm proud of myself. With photography, we can tell stories. We can express how we see the world.

Sol: So how has your idea of New York City changed?

Cyntia: Well, now I don't visit my family so often. *[Laughs.]* When they call and say, "Oh, come and visit us," I say, "You know what? I'm busy. I am taking my kids to the museum." Now I do believe that I'm a New Yorker. This is my home.

Sol: That makes me feel really good—and also emotional. I really hope that art can help my students be the best that they can, and that they discover their own power. Something that I have learned throughout the years is that the only person that can change you is yourself. And I feel like it's my duty to create spaces where these changes can happen.

Cyntia: Before I started your class, I was in a room with a closed door, and you opened the door for me. So I want to thank you—I thank you very much.

RECORDED IN NEW YORK, NEW YORK, ON JUNE 29, 2015.

Cyntia Gomar (*left*) and Sol Aramendi.

BEEKEEPER TED DENNARD, 43,
TALKS TO HIS FRIEND
CLAY CULVER, 35.

Ted Dennard: When I was about thirteen, there was an old man, Roy Hightower, who wanted to put his bees on my dad's land. In bee lingo, Roy needed a beeyard, and we had a good beeyard. It had gallberry and palmettos—just the right kind of flora. So my father said, "Fine, but teach us about beekeeping." So that's what he did.

On the weekends I would go out there and get in the beehives with old Roy. I would dress up in a raincoat and rain pants, and tuck them into my boots, and sweat my ever-living self off. I mean, the sweating part was awful, but the bee part was amazing. Roy was a man of not too many words, but I'd listen to everything he had to say, especially when I was in the bees with him. A lot of people actually confused him for my grandfather. He had white hair, and he always wore these little black-rimmed glasses; he was just this nice, totally even, well-mannered guy.

The first hive I opened up with Roy—just that sound, to have thousands of bees flying around, roaring and humming—it scared the *dickens* out of me. But to all of a sudden be in that world was cool, too. It was really neat to have what you would think is a dangerous animal all around you.

When we held a frame of honey up to the sun, I could see all the different-color honeys shining through. It was like stained glass; there was green and red and orange and yellow. And each one of those colors was because the bees went to the mint, or to the gallberry, or to the palmetto. And to actually be able to see and taste the differences—something about that totally hooked me. And it got into my blood.

Roy died a couple years after teaching me, and I kept his bees after that. And when I was in college, the guy I rented my place from had bees, and so I learned a lot more.

In the very beginning, I really tried to protect myself from getting stung. I would wear, like, battle gear—*dying* of heat, but I wasn't going to get stung! But I realized you're so much more careful and aware when you're not wearing a bunch of equipment. You really don't actually want to use gloves, because you end up killing so many bees that way. It's better just to get a sting. I sort of kept a rough count, but when I got to, I guess, twenty thousand stings, I quit counting. Once the fear went away and I realized I could always shut the top of the lid and walk away, that's when the joy really started.

Clay Culver: What is it about beekeeping that you love so much?

Ted: It's like rock climbing, or surfing: when you're doing it you don't think about anything else. When I'm beekeeping, I'm not thinking about dinner, or the past, or the future; I'm just totally in the moment. The sound and the sights—even the smell is just all-encompassing.

My favorite thing about bees is that they have this give-in-order-to-receive—or receive-in-order-to-give—way of living. And I mean, bees are 100 million years old; you can see on those old cave drawings from eight thousand years ago that man was collecting honey and getting stung.

I still have a whole lot to learn from bees. I'm more of a honey salesman now; I sold a few jars of honey to one store, then other stores called, and it's been sort of an avalanche of sales since then. It is a struggle, because I wasn't born business-minded, but I really try to emulate my business after a beehive, organization wise. It's a big little business for a beekeeper—and it's growing. But you know, after however many years it took me just to be calm in the beehive, that's also helped me be calm running this business. I try not to freak out, no matter what happens, and realize, *It's not as bad as you think it is.*

Clay: Have people ever told you you're crazy for doing this?

Ted: You know, my brother is famous for saying, "You can never make beekeeping work as a business." But I feel very fortunate, because it *has* worked—and I do feel like old Roy Hightower's controlling the show up there, pulling the strings. I wish I could talk to him today. I learned a lot.

RECORDED IN SAVANNAH, GEORGIA, ON FEBRUARY 17, 2009.

Clay Culver (*left*) and Ted Dennard.

JOSH GIPPIN, 33, TALKS WITH HIS GRANDMOTHER ROSE BRUDNO, 85, A BAR OWNER.

Josh Gippin: What were you doing in 1959?

Rose Brudno: I was disliking my husband intensely, and I was dumping him.

What I was really trying to do was find a way to support me and my three kids after I was divorced. So when I found this bar called the Zanzibar in Akron, I bought the place. When I took it over, the bar had all kinds of dirt and everything on the floor, but it was a corner bar in an important location, so I felt like it would be a good place for me to make a living.

I didn't realize it, but the nickname for the Zanzibar had been the "Bucket of Blood." And it earned that title—it was just a rough place. I got rid of the bouncer and I just told everybody, "If you're going to fight, you have to be able to back up your fight, because I'm not going to break it up." I really can't stand drunks. My theory is you lose on them anyway, so I eliminated drunks every chance I could. I just wanted a guy to cash his paycheck, buy a round of drinks, and then go home and take care of his family. That's how I operated.

The neighborhood was mostly rubber workers, who were one of the better unions, and they had a decent standard of living. A lot of them owned their own homes, they had good paychecks, and they could support having a drink or two. But I had some guys who were irresponsible with their money, and I knew they had families to support. So I would give them a twenty-dollar bill to party, and I just took their checks and put them in the safe.

Josh: So they would ask you to do that?

Rose: No, I just did it. Sure, they'd get mad—naturally. I mean, I'm doing a terrible thing: a guy works all week busting his butt, and someone has the audacity to take their money? They want to kill you. But then they would come in sheepishly later and get their paycheck and thank me. Because I was the only barkeep in town who would do that.

The Zanzibar was open from five thirty in the morning to two thirty in the morning—twenty-one hours. And I worked twelve-hour days.

Josh: How many customers are you going to get at five thirty in the morning?

Rose: Oh, lots, because at six o'clock they'd be coming off the graveyard shift, and they'd come in to eat breakfast. And at six o'clock in the morning we'd be singing and dancing and drinking and eating. Our cook, Lil, was the best in town. I brought my daughter Mindy's dinner every night from Lil's cooking.

You know, my dad had been an insurance man, but he had a heart condition, he was diabetic, and he was arthritic, so he couldn't work much. And when he did, he couldn't hold up. He got involved with the Unemployed Council, and he started helping unemployed workers when they were in trouble. Sometimes they would even stay at our house until they found a place to live and had the money to put up a month's rent to move.

And I had deep respect for that. I tried to organize a union in the bar. I said, "Hey, I'm not supposed to do this—I'm the enemy! You guys got to organize." But they wouldn't, so that's how I developed profit sharing. We took all the pennies from the bar, and by March we'd have about eight hundred, nine hundred dollars in the bank. Then we'd rent a big cottage for a month for the employees and their families to use for vacation in the summer.

We also had monthly meetings with all the barmaids about, *What is our role as a barmaid? When do we serve a drink, when do we deny a drink? How much respect do you give a guy, and when do you say, "You can't be here anymore"?*

If a barmaid felt that she had to bar someone for stuff like making sexual innuendos, I never questioned it—I backed her all the way. I had the best barmaids in town. Other barkeeps would try to buy my barmaids off by giving them a higher wage, but nobody left me. It was unheard of to have barmaids that worked for you ten, twelve years. But my barmaids never left.

Josh: I remember when I was thirteen years old, my girlfriend broke up with me and I was completely heartbroken—my eyes were swollen from crying. And you gave me a mop and a bucket and put me to work: "Start with the kitchen floors, and when you're done with those, come back, and I'll give you more." And it brought me down to earth. That's what it's always been like with you. You just told it like it was. People would say about you, "She's brazen and feisty and she won't take shit from people." *Crazy Rose*, they called you.

Rose: The guys used to say, "She's nuts!" you know. *[Laughs.]* But I experienced total support from the clientele.

Eventually the Zanzibar was designated for urban renewal, so I knew that it only had so much life left. And people were moving away from that area, and I was losing business. Plus, my back—just the stress of being on your feet all those hours. I had gotten so bad that my doctors said I had to quit. A couple of years later, it was emptied out. So that was that.

But you know, the period of the Zanzibar, those were the

best years of my life. I had a wonderful relationship with the community at the bar; I knew their kids, I knew their parents. We had a ball.

RECORDED IN AKRON, OHIO,
ON SEPTEMBER 2, 2009.

Rose Brudno passed away on June 29, 2011.

SALMON SLICER
LEONARD "LEN" BERK, 85,
TALKS WITH HIS FRIEND
JOSHUA GUBITZ, 46.

Leonard "Len" Berk: I never loved accounting, and I never thought that I was the best accountant out there. But it was important for me to make a living and take care of my children. My accounting career spanned twenty-five or thirty years. I decided to retire, and I was thinking, *What am I going to do next?*

I got a telephone call from a friend who said that she saw in *The New York Times* that Zabar's, a gourmet food store on West Eightieth Street and Broadway, was looking for a lox slicer, and I thought, *I could do that.* I had been a customer of that store for many years, and I would never have my lox sliced; I'd always buy a chunk and take it home and slice it myself. It's almost like I was preparing for this job.

So I sent the owner an email listing ten attributes that

would make me a fine lox slicer: "I'm reliable. I've been one of your best customers. I've always been a fish person."

Joshua Gubitz: You actually listed these?

Len: Yeah. I didn't really have any lox-slicing credentials, but I felt very comfortable with salmon. The owner called me immediately. "What kind of a CPA wants to slice lox?!" he said. "Well, we'll put you behind the counter and see what you can do."

When he decided that he would take me on, we sat down to negotiate. I was used to making $150 an hour. And he said, "How about nine dollars?" *[Laughter.]* But I've been slicing ever since.

When someone talks to me while I'm slicing, I don't respond. Somebody will say, "Do you hear what I'm saying?" And I say, "Yes, I do, but I'm very involved in slicing your salmon now." Some people, they're in a hurry. But you can't be in a hurry when you want to have salmon sliced.

Every time I slice, I want to make the best possible slice I can make. It's a sensual experience that occurs between me and my salmon and my knife, and I never get tired of it. It's mesmerizing. I'm always in the present moment when I'm slicing salmon. It's a very Zen thing. You can get lost in the lox. *[Laughs.]*

When I started, one of the things that I loved was my ability to deal with the most difficult customers. A customer would say, "I don't like that slice." I would say, "Oh, I'll be happy to take it off—and not only that, I'll give you a free slice!"

Or if I give people a taste of different salmons and they just can't find one that suits them, I'll say, "Don't worry about a thing. We have hundreds of salmons. We'll find one for you."

Joshua: What makes you want to be nice to those people?

Len: Well, I no longer want to be nice to them.

Joshua: [Laughs.] The Zen disappeared, huh?

Len: No. When I'm slicing, I'm slicing.

You know, I *like* lox, but I wouldn't say I love it. I would say I love *slicing* lox. I feel like I serve a really important function, at least, from the way some people carry on when they hear I don't have what they want; I must be doing something important! *[Laughter.]*

Now that I've been there for a while, I want my slices to have more style, more character—more *panache*. They look very lovely on the parchment, but they're not perfect.

The other day my wife came to me, and she said, "Have you ever thought about how you want to spend the rest of your life?" I said, "Yeah, I want to spend the rest of my life doing exactly what I'm doing: I want to slice salmon." I'm working toward the perfect slice.

RECORDED IN NEW YORK,
NEW YORK, ON MAY 13, 2015.

BEER VENDOR CLARENCE "CLANCY" HASKETT, 55, TALKS WITH HIS FRIEND AND FORMER COLLEAGUE JERRY COLLIER, 50.

Clarence "Clancy" Haskett: I used to play baseball in the streets with my friend John every single day, and we'd always listen to the baseball games on the radio. When we were fifteen, John started working at the stadium during the Orioles games, and then I went to work there with him, too. I always remember the date: June the seventh, 1974. I made $8.25 that day selling sodas. And from that very first day, I was hooked.

Jerry Collier: I met you probably the second day of my new job as a beer vendor—well, a *wannabe* beer vendor—at Memorial Stadium when I was nineteen years old. The Orioles won the World Series in '83, and I came in '84. And I fell in love with that job.

Clancy: When you came in, you was young—still in college. And you were selling your sodas, just plucking people off. They said, "Who is this guy?" They didn't even know your name. Next thing you know, you was in the top ten in sales. Next thing you know, you was in the top five. We gave you the name "the Terminator."

Jerry: Every vendor at the stadium was on a list that was ranked based on sales every twenty-seven games. There's an eighty-one-game season. And the person at the top of that list could pick what product they wanted to sell. And the best product in the stadium was beer.

Clancy: One of the guys, he had this little slogan that he started, and it went around all the vendors. So once you started working, he said, "What's gonna happen when they *revise . . . that . . . list?*" He used to say it a hundred times a day. *[Laughs.]* But it was a motivational tool for all of us.

Vendors would do little tricks and everything to sell more. I had the gift of gab, so that helped me out. I used to do rhymes, and everyone used to love those rhymes. It's just the type of job where you can't start off in slow motion. You have to always be aggressive. I was a Division I sprinter in college, and I used to race guys up and down the hallways. And since 1984, I've been consistently in the top five in sales. Next year will be thirty consecutive years.

Jerry: You were number one for a really long time, and I was number one for a really long time. So when you go into the stadium and you're at the top, you have incredible pressure on you to be a selling machine. I mean, the only thing that mattered was, "What's gonna happen when they *revise . . . that . . . list?*" *[Laughs.]* Because if you stop for a *second*, number five is coming. Number four is coming. And it's just perfect competition. It becomes almost like a sport.

Clancy: Well, that's the way that I look at it—my mind-set is like I'm a professional athlete. I have to stay in shape, I have to train during the off-season. Because vendors running around with straps around their neck? That's only on television commercials. Good vendors pick up their case and they carry it. Back in the old days we could carry five cases at a time.

Jerry: To be a vendor you've got to be athletic, personable, visible, fast—and be able to process a lot of information in your head. But we also had some vendors who weren't as athletic. One guy, he was working on an engineering degree from University of Maryland, and he created any number of mechanical devices to be able to pour beer faster. I mean, it was *stunning.* He went from being a middle-of-the-road vendor to being basically at the top.

Clancy: But I would say, "You don't need a can opener to sell beer; you need a personality!" And I *still* outsold them all. *[Laughs.]* But you know, we vendors competed against each other every single game, and we still hung out together.

Jerry: I would say it was like guys at any sporting event:

when you're in the heat of it, you're all in. But then when it was over … I mean, we've been on vacation together. You were in my wedding. I was in yours. I've been in two handfuls of vendors' weddings! Love them like they're brothers.

From my perspective, if you're really good at this, you're good at it because you love it. And it's consuming. Put it this way: how did we plan our weddings?

Clancy: Around the Orioles' schedule.

Jerry: [Laughter.] That's true. To miss a game, the stress levels weren't worth it. And when you get to that level, it's in your soul.

I left in June of '96 because my first son was born, and I got promoted at my other job. I struggled, because I loved vending. But the hardest part was leaving that place and not being able to see you guys every single day.

When I first arrived at the stadium and looked around the ballpark, you were just this ray of sunshine: a guy who outworked people, who loved all the customers more than anybody else. You were so positive, and you just *crushed* it. And I said, "That's who I want to be."

I mean, you're larger than life in a lot of ways. But I know there's another side of you—more than the rhymes and all that.

Clancy: Right, yeah. My mother died ten days after I was born, and since my father was working a lot, my grandmother became my guardian. I ended up moving back with my father when I was five or six, and everything that I did—the littlest thing—I got a beating for. It was just war. Just before I turned nine, my father beat me with an extension cord, and it left large welts on my forehead. My friend saw it on a Saturday, and when I got to school on Monday, they took me out of class and asked, "What is going on with your head?" And I told them how I got it. They packed up my bags, and I moved in with my aunt that day.

That was probably *the* turning point in my entire life. I got around people who loved and cared about me. It changed my life. And it helped me think about things before I did them. Instead of being hotheaded, you know, I just don't go there.

Jerry: Well, you epitomize to me all that's right in the world. You're a great man. And hearing how you grew up helps me to have a deeper understanding for *why* you see things the way you do. So if it's a rainout at the Orioles game and you only sell two cases of beer, in the big scheme of life, that's not even a setback.

Clancy: No, that's not a problem at all.

I feel good. And so as long as I'm still healthy, I'll put in another good ten years. That's going to be fifty years of vending.

Wherever I am, I can go in a restaurant or a bar that I've never been in before, and somebody say, "Send that guy over there a beer!"

Jerry: That's something I miss. You sit in a restaurant and all these people come up to you, you know? Nobody knows me anymore. I'm just a boring banker now.
[Laughter.]

RECORDED IN BALTIMORE, MARYLAND,
ON DECEMBER 9, 2014.

Clarence Haskett (*left*) and Jerry Collier.

ENTERTAINER COACH OPERATOR
ARNIE KNAPP, 53,
TALKS WITH HIS WIFE,
JUDY KNAPP, 48.

Arnie Knapp: I have driven coach buses for different bands and artists over the years, and I've always said *there's no band that I know of that tours more than I do.* I don't go out for just two or three months: for decades now—my whole career—I have been on the road over three hundred days a year. I've probably got close to three million miles logged now; been to all fifty states and throughout Canada. And so when it comes to traveling out on the road, I know what I'm talking about.

Judy Knapp: We met in Los Angeles while I was singing alto for a group called the Heritage Singers. You had hopped on our tour bus to drive it, and I remember you had on a pair of red shorts and an aqua shirt, and you had on a gold chain with an eagle. You were very svelte back then. Now you have this long, silvery hair down to the middle of your back, but back then your hair was short. You looked like the very good Baptist boy. And my little Christian, good-girl heart went, *Ooh, he's kind of hot. [Laughs.]* This was December of '88, and we got married in '90. Then we had our son, Greg, and our daughters, Savannah and Jaylen.

In the beginning, we did have our struggles trying to mold two lives together. I was a singer, and you were a bus driver, which took you away from home.

Arnie: In our twenty-five years, the most time that we've ever spent together in a single block of time is about six weeks. I have actually been on a tour where we've gone within a mile of our house on the freeway and I hadn't seen you and the kids in weeks, and the toughest part was knowing that I couldn't stop.

Judy: I got through a lot of it when we were first trying to adjust because I was very involved in church. But when I think about it, it's probably a good thing that I didn't listen too often to what the preachers were preaching. *[Laughs.]* You know, "A good husband will be at home." I had no intention of demolishing our family because your job took you away.

Wives with touring husbands, we're called "road widows." There are so many road musicians, crew, road managers, and when these cats leave for tours, their wives are all living the same life. Here in Nashville, it's very common. So I can handle it, but there are times I crawl in bed and I would like you there.

Arnie: I believe a lot of folks think, "Man, this is glamorous—out with some of the biggest names on the planet!" But you know what? You can be in these huge crowds where there are sold-out stadiums, and while you're waiting for your people to get onto your bus, your mind is just back home. I get tired of eating by myself.

Judy: But be honest: when you've been home long, you're like "I need to get my butt back on the road." *[Laughs.]* You're a nomad—you like to wander and travel. And it's not just the traveling bug; it's the *need* for the view of the office to change every day. You can sit for about five days and then the pulsing begins. I can see it start to radiate off your body. And the vein pops and I'm like, "OK, you need to go. You need to go now!" *[Laughs.]*

But I can honestly say that you've always been a hands-on dad. When our kids had issues, especially during the middle school years, you would fly home, put a suit on, and you'd walk into that school like the boss. And so your kids knew that if they needed you, you showed up.

Arnie: Whenever I first meet the artists that I'm driving for, I always try to get acquainted with them and tell them a little bit about myself. And then I let them know, "Look, I'm the most important part of this outfit as far as I'm concerned, because I have to keep all of you folks safe while we're going down the highway to make it to the next gig. I've got a wonderful wife and three beautiful children to go back home to. And if I do something stupid up here, if I don't get enough sleep, I put my family at risk." So I take my responsibilities very seriously. That's always in the back of my mind when I'm driving these million-dollar machines down the road.

It's only now, after almost two and a half decades of marriage, that I'm beginning to understand the incredible amount of stuff that you had to do on your own. I feel very fortunate to have you as my wife, because I know so many other drivers that are on their second, third, and fourth marriages. This industry doesn't really nurture strong relationships.

Judy: Well, I think we were designed to do it this way. After twenty-five years, I'd only say one year was a throwaway. For the most part, I think we've grown like a real good comfortable pair of shoes. *[Laughter.]*

Arnie: Tonight, I'm heading out to Miami, and I'll be gone for a month. And I've only had a day here with you from the last tour. And you know, I'm getting to the age now where I've done this for so long, at some point I've got to hang it up. But as long as I can pass the physical, and you allow me to do this, I will.

I've observed that when you're touring, all artists are the same—I don't care if you sing country, if you do gospel music, if you're an ice-skater. As much as everybody likes to tour, it's a love-hate relationship. Everybody loves to go home, but then

after they're home for a while, they can't wait to get back out and go do it again.

RECORDED IN NASHVILLE, TENNESSEE,
ON OCTOBER 14, 2014.

SUBWAY CONDUCTOR
PAQUITA WILLIAMS, 55, TALKS
WITH HER PASSENGER
LAURA LANE, 28.

Paquita Williams: I was born in New York City, in Queens, the second of eight children. I grew up thinking I was going to be a famous fashion designer. I had a godmother, Ann, and I used to tell my mother, "When I grow up, I'm going to be just like Ann," because I thought she was a designer. But Ann worked in a cleaner's—she did the mending there. *[Laughter.]*

I graduated from high school and I went on to FIT and studied patternmaking. I worked with a big designer and I worked in a lot of sample rooms, so I really thought I was going to be in that arena. Because at FIT, they just set you up to believe you're going to be the next big thing—there was no limit. They didn't say "Well, you might" or "You can't." But then when the season finished, I would be out of a job.

About ten years ago, I took a test for the city jobs. Maybe three or four years later, they called me, and I went to Transit. It was a good opportunity: it gave me job security, and I was able to pay my bills. You know, working where I *might* have a job once the line is finished—it's no guarantee. But one thing that is guaranteed: each and every month the landlord wants the rent.

So I started off as a token booth clerk. And then in February of 2001, I was hired as a conductor, and my first job was on the F line. You'd have people that would stand at the same door every single day, so sometimes I'd see the same people riding in my train. And then I really started noticing them. They would see me and say, "Good morning, hi!" And I realized, *People know me because I'm the conductor.* I remember the first day I had stopped smoking; it was *rough*. But I had people on the train coming back the next day: "How you doing with the cigarettes?" And that makes my day better.

Laura Lane: I met you when we got stopped underground for two hours.

Paquita: We were on the A train at nine o'clock in the morning. We had just left Fifty-Ninth Street when—we found out later—the power went out. There was no power on the tracks, north or south. So as a conductor, I have my announcement that I make through the train on the public announcement system: "Ladies and gentlemen, we're being held momentarily.

The train operator's checking things out at this time; hopefully we'll be moving shortly."

And every five or ten minutes, I kept letting the passengers know that we are checking it out. But after a while, I knew somebody would be nervous. Passengers get a little antsy when you don't see anyone in authority and don't know what's going on. So I put on my bright orange vest and opened my cab door to just let the people know, *I'm here.*

I walked through the whole train from front to back and just calmed people down. Passengers were saying to me, "It's Friday the thirteenth!" I said, "Well, we're alive to see Friday the thirteenth. Somebody didn't wake up on Friday the thirteenth and would have loved to have been on this train. So it's a good day for us!"

Laura: I think you just kind of put everything in perspective. And you were hilarious—just joking back and forth with the people in my car. Then everyone started laughing.

Even after we had gotten out, you were going out of your way. As I was leaving, you said, "If you need a note for work, this is where you find it."

So what could have started out as a bad day turned into a good day because of you. You made everybody on that train start talking with each other like human beings; we connected. I've been in New York for five years and never talked to strangers like that. It was just a great feeling. I left the train and somebody was like, "Let's do this again tomorrow morning—same place, same time!" And I would've.

Paquita: No, let's not! *[Laughter.]* You know, about twenty years ago, I went to the dentist, and I was so afraid. And I said to the dentist, "Please, *please*, hold my hand. Just let me know you're there." And he said to me, "No, I'm not your date."

That stuck with me, and that's the reason I do what I do with my passengers. When you get on my train and something's going on, I want you to know that I'm not running off

without you. I'm putting on my orange vest and letting you know that if you need me to hold your hand, I'm right there.

RECORDED IN NEW YORK, NEW YORK, ON OCTOBER 7, 2013.

Paquita Williams (*left*) and Laura Lane.

SYDNEY REED, 10,
TALKS WITH HER GRANDFATHER
JIM CLYBURN, 66,
A CONGRESSMAN.

Sydney Reed: In your lifetime, have you ever wanted to do any other job than politics?

Jim Clyburn: No, never wanted to do anything else. I enjoy the give-and-take of politics. I love to campaign, and I love meeting people. Going around the country, you learn a lot. I was always involved in politics. I was very active in the sit-ins. In fact, I met your grandmother in 1957, when we were students at South Carolina State and we were demonstrating against segregation.

The first time I was arrested, I was in jail pretty much all day. In the early evening, all of us were gathered in this big courtroom, waiting on bail to be posted. Your grandmother came in with some of her friends, and I started talking about how hungry I was. A little while later, she disappeared. And she came back holding a hamburger. And when she presented me with the hamburger, I reached for it—but she pulled it back. Then she broke the hamburger in half, gave me a half, and she ate the other half. And that's how we met. About a year and a half later, we got married.

Sydney: So, have you ever felt you wanted to quit?

Jim: Oh, absolutely. I'll tell you a story. When I won the primary of the South Carolina house of representatives in June of 1970, there was this big party after the votes came in, and everybody was jumping up and down and very happy that we won. But the next morning, I went into the bathroom, and there on my sink was a little note from your grandmother: "When you win, brag gently. When you lose, weep softly." And I just took it and I stuck it up on the mirror.

We got into the general election in November, and when the polls closed that evening, all the news media announced that I had gotten elected. But then somebody rang my doorbell at about three thirty in the morning and told me that something had gone wrong down at the courthouse. I went down there and they told me, "Rather than winning by five hundred votes, we have determined that you have lost by five hundred votes."

So the next morning when I went to my bathroom, I looked up at the mirror and I wept softly. I thought that this was the worst thing that could possibly happen. But I gathered my wits, and I determined that I was going to go forward.

I ran for secretary of state in 1978, and lost. Eight years later, in 1986, I ran for secretary of state *again*—and lost. And more than one person said to me, "Well, that's your third strike. What are you going to do next?" And I always said to people, "Three strikes may be an out in baseball, but life is not baseball." And I just never gave up. And so in 1992, six years after I lost the second secretary of state race, I ran for the United States Congress. And this time I won.

There was just something that kept telling me, *You can't throw in the towel. You've got to stick this out.* You know, on our state seal in South Carolina we have a Latin phrase that says, *Dum Spiro Spero*—"While I breathe, I hope." And I've always felt that wher-ever there's life, there's hope. I never gave up. I kept running for office until I got it right.

RECORDED IN COLUMBIA, SOUTH CAROLINA,
ON FEBRUARY 9, 2007.

EMPLOYMENT COUNSELOR DARLENE LEWIS, 60, TALKS WITH HER EMPLOYEE AND FRIEND JAMES TAYLOR, 40.

Darlene Lewis: I've always worked with young people. Way back in 1985, I was the president of a PTA, and I realized the young people were being passed along without actually knowing how to go out and get a job; my son had that problem, too. So I started teaching these eleventh- and twelfth-graders how to fill out an application, how to do interviews, and it was so rewarding for me to see how many made the right choices because they had a second chance.

After about four years, this boy, eighteen years old, came to me after he went to prison for aggravated robbery. He only stayed ten months, but when he got out it was very difficult to find him a job. Well, the seventeen years I had spent at Wendy's paid off, because I was able to call the manager and get her to hire him.

So I started specializing in working with guys with a felony background who had difficulties finding employment. That was thirty years ago, and it's still going.

James Taylor: At seventeen, I was sentenced to thirteen years in prison, and I served seven. I felt out of touch with society, so I did a lot of reading, a lot of studying in there, and I got my GED. When I got out, I was eager to have another chance—but I thought that I was seven years behind everybody else, and I felt like I had to make up for that, and so that had me in a rush.

When I got out, I did a lot of applications, and I got a lot of noes. Even if there was a "We're Hiring" sticker on the window, they still would find a way to tell me no. I was out for a while, and I was battered and broken from trying to find a job—until I met you, Miss Lewis.

I remember when I first came in. You sat me down, and you found out what I was *trying* to do. And if I couldn't do what I was trying to do, what would I like to do then? And then we started to search. The first job that you sent me to was McDonald's. I worked there for two years and became a manager.

Over the years, when I'd fall and want to give up, you'd be right there waiting to pick me up and send me somewhere else.

It was a tough road, and I probably couldn't have made it if you weren't there to help me.

Darlene: What are you most proud of since getting out?

James: I always told you that I wanted to help people like me. Because the streets is an easy out for people who feel frustrated with what we call "normal society." And now I'm working with you on a teen program we created.

We took the kids to Cocoa Beach, Florida, for a week. Half of them hadn't ever even been out of Little Rock. They're kids out of the neighborhood—poverty-stricken, single-parent children, like I was. So to see the looks on their faces when they saw the sunset over the ocean for the first time when we went walking out on the beach, I knew then that this is what I was meant to do.

Darlene: Right now we've got about thirty kids, and I'm Grandma to every one of them. And you're like a father to those children. They come to you when they got problems.

James: Well, I can relate to the young guys. They respect me and look up to me because I know what they're going through. When I was young, my father and my mother weren't there, and so the other children in the neighborhood became my family support—but their minds was just as mixed up as mine. So I can say to these guys now, "Dude, this is how you feeling, right?" Because I know: children get into what they get into because they feel like that's all they can do.

And so I commend you, because I sit and watch some of

them come in, and I can see the *non*-gratitude on their face. And you still feed people, you clothe them. You take your time with them.

Have you ever felt like quitting?

Darlene: No, never. Sometimes I've felt like saying, *Oh God, Darlene. You get up every morning and go there every day. Is the community ever going to realize that these are our children and we need to jump in and help?* In thirty years it hasn't gotten any better. But I'm still doing it.

James: I know people are waiting for me to go back to the streets and sell drugs. If I'm not doing so well—my car may be broke down or I need something—it's always, "He'll be back," because I know what quick money is, and they don't believe that I've changed.

But I look in the mirror every morning, and I like what I see. I feel like I'm a good father and a good person. I'll go through anything to keep this change, because if those young boys in the neighborhood were to see me in the hood selling drugs, it would crush them.

Darlene: Well, James, from the first day I met you, I knew you were going to make it, because of your heart. There were so many places you wanted to go, and it was going to take a little time, but I knew that if you kept going, you'd succeed in life.

During the time that we've known each other, do you ever feel like I've been too hard on you?

James: Yeah. But I've felt what it feels like for somebody to be hard on you and they don't care at all. In prison, they didn't care. When you're hard on me, it's *love* in it. I talk loud. I'm short-tempered. But from day one, you have accepted me. And I love you to death for it.

Darlene: What I admire about you is your willingness to *stick.* You have the spirit to do whatever's necessary to make

things work, and you put 110 percent into what you do. So I am very proud to have you in my life. We make a good team.

James: Yes, ma'am, we do.

RECORDED IN LITTLE ROCK, ARKANSAS, ON NOVEMBER 24, 2014.

WAITRESS AND BLUES SINGER
MIRANDA LOUISE, 57.

Miranda Louise: I've worked at Brown's Diner in Nashville for twenty-two years now. It's one of the oldest restaurants in the whole state of Tennessee, been there since 1927. And it's the greatest place in the world.

I came to Nashville to sing blues music in 1981. Brown's gave me a daytime spot a few days a week during the week, so I could leave Thursday and go do my gigs and come back Sunday. It's really hard to find any job where you have that kind of flexibility. If you work for any of these chain restaurants and you say, "I've got a gig in Paris for three weeks, and I've got to go," they'd just say, "Have fun—hope you find a job when you come home." But Brown's gave me the opportunity to keep doing the music that I love.

There's thirteen of us that run Brown's—thinkers and artists and songwriters and musicians, people who don't necessarily want to wear a suit and a tie. We don't advertise—never, ever. We don't have T-shirts or matches that say "Brown's" on them. We don't even have a computer. And there's no turnover: either you're liked and trusted, or you don't get hired.

When I first got to Brown's, I found out that people don't want to feel like they're being waited on. They want it to be more like their house. So now when I see people I know walk in, I'll turn their order in once I see where they decided to sit. It's almost like people just discovered they can get taken care of in the second living room they didn't know they had. And when they're comfortable, they're coming back.

Now, today's Tuesday, and I know there'll be Larry, Greg Lebleu, Francis. There'll be Joe—he's the minister on death row. There'll be a few others probably, and many of them have been going to Brown's for over twenty-five years. And then there'll be a boatload more people that I know but don't necessarily know their names.

There's a whole way of life that's based around this place. Even the owner treats me just like a cousin or something; he treats all of us that way. I don't know about you, but most of the people I know can't say that their boss tells them that they love them, and I don't mean anything but in the most Christian way.

Some of us have had health issues; some of us have had financial issues. I have a coworker that's losing her vision, and I told her that if they take away her license, I'll pick her up in the morning and take her in and open with her. We don't throw people away at Brown's. The only reason people leave is because they die.

I think all of us at Brown's feel we have a responsibility to do the job that we have to do, because otherwise it could fall apart. Brown's could turn into a parking lot. I mean, we're held together by duct tape and chewing gum *[laughs]*, and if it's broken, you're fixing it, because we're not getting anything new. If you want to keep a place going this long, that's what the mentality has to be. But we've survived World War II, the Korean War, the Vietnam War, double-dip recession—all those things going on in the world around us.

So I would say that if you're lucky enough to walk into a situation in which you fit, recognize it. Because there's nothing worse than saying what might have been. Recognizing that also made me realize that it's the same with relationships, friends, love life, finances—everything. As soon as you recognize it, grab it. Stay there.

RECORDED IN NASHVILLE, TENNESSEE,
ON OCTOBER 14, 2014.

| V |

GROUNDBREAKERS

MARC ANDERSON LAWSON, 42, TALKS WITH HIS SISTER, KAREN LAWSON, 45, ABOUT THEIR FATHER, VIDEO GAME INVENTOR JERRY LAWSON.

Marc Anderson Lawson: Growing up, no matter where you were in our house, you could hear Dad's keys jingle at the door. And as soon as we heard that, we would just get up from wherever we were and run to hug Dad. He'd pick us up and pretend like he was King Kong: "Aaaahhhh!" *[Laughter.]* He was a big kid.

Karen Lawson: [Laughs.] Yeah, he was. Our dad was six foot six—I mean, he walks into a room and he's filling up the doorway. And he was a great storyteller. He would have folks hanging on his words. And he told it to you straight, no chase. He'd say, "The truth is the truth, and the world doesn't sugarcoat it for you, so I'm not going to do that in my own home."

Marc: Dad grew up in the South Jamaica, Queens, projects,

which was a rough environment. But my grandfather was really big into science, and he got my father interested in science, too. Dad was always into doing things that were different. He got into electronics at an early age, and he started fixing television sets when he was, like, sixteen or seventeen years old. He talked a lot about how his teacher sat him next to a poster of George Washington Carver and said, "You can be this great!"

He went to Queens College for about a year or two, and then left and went out to Palo Alto, California, to pursue what he loved.

Karen: He had a natural curiosity for things that ticked and moved—he was a tinkerer. And that grew into a career. When we were kids, our father invented the first cartridge-based home video game system, called the Fairchild Channel F. I mean, his intelligence was off the charts.

Marc: We grew up in a suburb of San Francisco called Santa Clara, and some of my earliest memories are of us playing video games together on the Channel F. There was *Maze*, *Blackjack*—*Tic-Tac-Toe* was a fun one, too. If you lost, at the bottom it would say, "You lose, Turkey"! That was Dad's thing. *[Laughs.]* We never knew till we were grown that we were really just debugging the games. He was like, "Just give them to the kids and let them play." He got some free labor out of us! *[Laughs.]*

But you know, when you think about it, we were some of the first children—really, *the* first kids—to play interchangeable cartridges on a video game system on the planet Earth. Because this was a year prior to Atari coming out—so this was historic. But I mean, our friends would just come over and we'd play these games.

Dad had this huge lab in our garage. You ever see an episode of *Star Trek* where you see everyone sitting around the consoles? That's what the lab looked like to me as a child. There was a computer about the size of a refrigerator called a PDP-11, with big tape wheels on it that spun around. And then there might be eight to ten other computers, all working on different things networked together. And just electronic parts all over the place. Because Dad was not only constructing things; he would also take things apart to see how they were done.

I used to be embarrassed because when my friends would come over, they would see all this equipment in there and be like, "What the hell is that stuff?" And then we had maybe five or six large antennas outside the house, and people were like, "What are you guys trying to do, launch a satellite or something?!"

But you know, his work was his hobby, and his hobby was his work. And I think that had a lot of influence on me.

I remember the summer our cousin Manu came, and all we wanted to do was play video games. But Dad took them away, and he gave us a book on how to program video games—and he *forced* us to figure out how to make our own games. *Mad Libs* was really big around that time, so Manu and I made a

Mad Libs game using one of the computers Dad had. It actually worked! We thought it was so cool. I must have been twelve, but just that *one* summer, it changed the whole trajectory of my life.

So when I first went to college, I was like, *What could I do for a living that I would want to do for free?* I thought about it and I said, *Well, I like to program. I'd do that for free.* And that's what made me get into software development.

Karen: Wow, I never knew that. But I think that speaks to Dad's personality and who he was.

Marc: Yeah, I always felt an inner drive to do great because of him. He would help me through a lot of the projects that I was working on, and it was exciting because we had this bond.

When I finished graduate school and started looking for work, I ended up getting a great opportunity, and I said, "OK, this is it." I told Mom and Dad both about the interview, and they were excited for me; Dad was *really* excited. He's like, "You'll get the job."

Karen: And he was right.

Marc: Yeah, but he just didn't get to see the end result.

Dad was a diabetic, and there was a point where he was really sick and he had to stop working. He eventually had to have his leg amputated just below the knee, and then went into a wheelchair—and I think that had a huge effect on him. His eyesight also started to fail because he had macular degeneration, and he lost one of his eyes. So now he only has one eye, one leg—and he had to move around in a wheelchair. Well, that's pretty difficult when you're used to doing a lot of things on your own. Then the doctor said something about him having to lose the other leg, and having to have kidney dialysis. So that would have meant that he would spend a majority of his waking hours doing the dialysis. And because he's so mathematical, Dad figured out that he'd only have *one* quality hour per day. I remember he said to me, "What kind of life is that?" He said he'd rather go. And he passed away in 2011.

Karen: When he did pass, as sad as it was, we both knew that he lived a full life. Dad was a man without limitations as far as what he felt he could accomplish.

Marc: And he was a man who went his own path. If everyone was going right, he'd figure out a good reason to go left. That was just him. He created his own destiny, and that's a fantastic legacy.

RECORDED IN ATLANTA, GEORGIA, ON OCTOBER 12, 2014.

COUNTY CLERK
CLELA ROREX, 71, TALKS WITH
HER FRIEND SUE LARSON, 57.

Clela Rorex: In 1974 there was a county clerk election here in Boulder. There had been no woman in that office for over thirty years, and it pissed me off. And so my friend said, "Well, why don't you run for office?" So I did.

I was thirty-one years old, and the campaign was pretty difficult for me. I don't know how I made it, because I was just an anomaly: I looked young, I had long hair, and I wore miniskirts; a local paper characterized me as a Barbie doll. *[Laughter.]* But much to my surprise, I won, and I was sworn in on January 14th of '75.

On the surface the county clerk has a very boring job. *[Laughs.]* It varies some by state, but in Colorado the clerk is charged with issuing marriage licenses and license plates, with recording documents, and with managing the voting. But in

'74 Boulder passed the first ordinance of any municipality in the country to try to protect the rights of gays and lesbians, and it created a furor.

In March 1975, a gay couple came to my door to get a marriage license; it was the first time I met openly gay people. They lived in Colorado Springs, and when they went to the clerk there, she said, "We don't do that here. Go to Boulder."

But when they came in I said, "I don't know if I can do this either. I need a couple of days to find out." I was told that the Colorado marriage code did not specify that marriage had to be between a man and a woman. So when they came back I said, "You're on legal grounds if you want to do this. It's your decision."

I was very naive politically, so I felt like it was simply a matter of fairness and equity and right and wrong. It wasn't forbidden by law, and therefore I did it. But I had absolutely no real comprehension of the kind of wrath that I would bring down on myself.

Sue Larson: Yeah, Boulder was a different place than it is now. I'm sure you got plenty of hate mail.

Clela: I had entire church congregations writing me, saying I was creating Sodom and Gomorrah in the area; that all the gays in the world would migrate to Boulder and that it would ruin everybody's property values.

One day I was in my office looking out my window, and this horse trailer drives up with some media vans. Then this cowboy gets out with his horse. And all of a sudden it just dawned on me: *He's going to ask for a marriage license for his horse.* And so my deputy and I started flipping through the marriage code like crazy. You know, *What are we going to do?!*

So he comes in, asks for a marriage license, and I went to the counter and started taking his information. I ask him his name and his horse's name, which was Dolly. And I said, "How old is Dolly?" He said, "Eight, I think." And I put my pen down, just calm as could be—how, I don't know. And I said, "Well, I'm sorry, but that's too young to get a license without parental approval." That story hit the world, and my actions made me a laughingstock for many people.

Sue: So how many couples came to Boulder and were married by you?

Clela: After the first couple from Colorado Springs, I issued five more licenses. But it was really hard on me. I honestly did not anticipate the degree of hate. It was threats. I mean, people wanted to kill me for doing this. I had a small son and people would call on the phone and if he answered they would spiel their hatred to him. And I was scared. So I didn't see through my term in office. I was disappointed, because I wanted to.

Sue: Well, there are some people out here who know what a big deal that was and what a stand you took. I mean, I remember being in high school then, hearing about this new county clerk we had elected who came along and started marrying gay people. I was sixteen or seventeen and was too young to vote, but in my gut I knew, *This is something that affects you.* I didn't know what I was yet, but I knew what I wasn't.

I remember just watching and being surprised that teachers I really respected had started talking about gay people in not a very nice way. I'm like, *Why would you say that about these people?* Not knowing I was one of those people. And then, oh, ten years later, I figured it out. *[Laughter.]*

In Boulder at that time, no one was coming out—or even hardly talking about it—even through the eighties. And so to offer support for anything even remotely gay-oriented—it just blew me away. And years ago didn't you go down to Denver and presided over dozens of same-sex couples who had a symbolic marriage ceremony?

Clela: They couldn't get an elected official to say the vows, so they called me. That was actually one of the most emotional moments that I've had through all of this. The couples were there in droves—every stripe and color. Every type of dress you can imagine. Some in very formal wedding gowns and others not. They said their vows to each other, and they would always say how long they'd been together. I mean, many of them had been together for decades—they had lived their entire lives together.

Sue: Well, we have some pretty incredible allies in this town, and you're one of them. You're certainly one of my heroes.

Clela: [Laughs.] Thanks, Sue, but I don't feel like a hero. I just was a young woman who tried to do the right thing. And given the same circumstances, I would do it again. I feel like that decision changed my life in many ways, and thank good-

ness I made it, because it would be so hard for me to look myself in the mirror today if I hadn't.

RECORDED IN BOULDER, COLORADO, ON MAY 22, 2014.

Sue Larson (left) and Clela Rorex.

REVEREND ERIC D. WILLIAMS, 54, TALKS TO HIS COLLEAGUE JANNETTE BERKELEY-PATTON, 46.

Eric D. Williams: **Eighteen or nineteen years ago, I got a call from a local funeral home. She said, "Pastor, I've got a really big favor to ask. There's a kid, been a member of his church all his life, and he's died of AIDS and his pastor won't do the funeral."** He was twenty-six years old, and he just happened to be gay. She said that when the pastor of the church found out how he died, he just said, "The funeral can't happen in our church."

Pastoral life in Kansas City is a very small fraternity, and it's not appropriate for one pastor to go against what another pastor has said. So I really didn't want to do the funeral. I was a young pastor with a very small church, and there was a pecking order: the older guys with the bigger churches were the ones whose voices were heard. I was just supposed to mind my own business and not meddle with this. And I was perfectly all right with that—until I went home and really started thinking about this family.

The Bible tells us that we're not supposed to do what everybody else does. And the fact that this pastor was so afraid of his own congregation getting up and walking away that he couldn't support this family in their darkest hour of need was wrong. So I did the funeral.

I met the parents of this kid, and I was used to black dads disowning their gay sons—but not this family. They celebrated their son's life—just unconditional love. There were some pretty flamboyant characters there, but they didn't shake Dad. This father and this mother were so welcoming to his friends. They taught me more in that little experience than any of the Sunday school books or the courses in seminary.

African American people, some of us don't like to talk about sensitive stuff. We think that if you talk about it, it's going to spread—or that there's a lightning bolt that's going to come out of the sky and just zap you. So you avoid airing your "dirty laundry." But HIV/AIDS was affecting us, and nobody was reaching out. And so I had to do *something*—and telling people the truth, putting it in people's faces, seemed like the thing to do. And so we started educating people.

When the clergy in Kansas City heard what we were doing, people withdrew their fellowships from us. They thought either my wife or I had AIDS and it was going to rub off on them, or that I was gay and would proposition them. I still remember being at one ministers' conference, and at lunchtime I went to join a few fellow pastors, and when I sat down at the table everybody got up and walked away.

But over the years it's evolved. And as people have had losses of their own, they began to trust us for information. We're not trying to change theology—we don't get into debates about whether homosexuality is right or wrong—we just want them to know they've got a shoulder to lean on.

I came into this work kicking and screaming. *[Laughs.]* I just didn't want to do it. But my heart was pulled. Everything good that I've been able to accomplish in ministry has started with some kind of a burden, and AIDS *burdened* me.

I'm not a real vocal or boisterous person; I was always one of those kids that would sit in a corner and try not to get noticed. But this call, these burdens really force you to do stuff that you don't even think you have the skill to do. And you know, in being vocal, you take hits. I've lost people I thought were friends doing this work. But no one should have to bury their kid; you're not supposed to have to do that. Doing that funeral for that family was the event that rearranged my whole life.

RECORDED IN KANSAS CITY, MISSOURI, ON SEPTEMBER 27, 2010.

CHEF AND RESTAURATEUR
LAURA MARTINEZ, 30, TALKS
WITH HER BUSINESS ADVISER,
ANDREW FOGATY, 57.

Laura Martinez: At the age of one, I was diagnosed with cancer tumors in both of my eyes. They couldn't survive all of the heavy treatment and radiation, so they took out my right eye, leaving in my left. I used to see shadows and light, but with all the surgeries I had throughout the years, it pretty much killed the little light perception I had. Now I don't see anything.

I was a very active kid. I'm originally from Guanajuato, Mexico, and my house there had these big trees that I climbed with my cousins. I was a dangerous girl *[laughs]*; my mom let me have this knife that I always played with. It was pretty dull, but I used it to chop sticks off the trees and pretend I was a butcher or something.

I was always exploring my surroundings, and whenever I

heard my grandma and my mother and aunts cooking, I would go in and play with the dough for the tortillas, or whatever they had. And the *smells*! They made mole with all these toasty peppers and spices, and when they grind it you could just smell the oils from the nuts. Just awesome smells. It was incredible.

Andrew Fogaty: And then eventually your family moved to the U.S., right? To Illinois?

Laura: Yeah, to Moline, when I was nine. I didn't know any English, no braille, and I had no schooling, because the town where we lived in Mexico didn't have any special schools for me. There was one four hours away, but it cost money, and my mom didn't have that.

So I had to learn everything from scratch here. I felt lost because I didn't understand the language, and I wasn't used to the schools. I was a good learner, but I couldn't sit still. I always got yelled at because I was always feeling around and sometimes I knocked over my teacher's coffee or something. *[Laughs.]* And so I had to learn how to keep my hands still.

My family always treated me normal. I didn't even know that I was blind; I just thought everybody saw the way I did. It wasn't until junior high that my family sat me down and explained to me that I couldn't see.

Andrew: So then what brought you to Chicago?

Laura: Moline is a very small city. It doesn't have much access for people with disabilities, and I wanted to be more independent, more capable of myself. I wanted something bigger. I always contemplated the idea of being a chef, and at twenty-five, I moved to Chicago to go to Le Cordon Bleu.

I got accepted into the school, but it was not easy. They kept saying that they lost my paperwork. Eventually I talked to someone in the president's office and explained to him what was going on. He said to me that his mom was blind, too, but he didn't think his mother was capable of doing something like cooking at Le Cordon Bleu. I said, "How do you know?" I was like, "Give me a chance. And if I'm not able to succeed here, I will pick up my things and leave—you won't even have to kick me out." In the end he backed off. I stayed and proved to everybody that I could do it—and I graduated.

I started working for Chef Charlie Trotter, which was a big honor, because he was our role model in school. And it was a great experience—hard work, fast pace. It was my first real job, and it was fun. I worked for him for about three years, until he announced on New Year's Eve that he was closing his restaurant.

After that, I went on *many* job interviews, and no luck. Nobody cared who I worked with, what I did, or where I studied. They just saw that I was blind. Well, I got kind of bored with that. I needed a job, or I needed to start working on my dream: opening my own restaurant. And so I was just like, *Who's going to help me?*

I did the research on assistance with small business, and that's where I found you. I remember calling you and saying,

"This is Chef Martinez. I would like to schedule an appointment with you. Is that possible?"

Andrew: When you called, you did not sound very happy. You just sounded fed up; it was the tone of somebody speaking through gritted teeth. So I was *not* looking forward to that appointment. *[Laughs.]* I thought that it might be a bit of a battle.

Laura: I think my first meeting with you was a little intimidating, because I didn't tell you that I was blind. I was afraid that if I said I was, you would hang up. So I guess it was a little shocking for you when I came in.

Andrew: I thought it was surprising, but no, I wasn't shocked. I'd never met a blind chef, but I didn't know how unusual it was at that point. And then very quickly you relaxed a little bit and we started talking.

It was very clear that you were skilled. You had the background: you'd worked at Trotter's. You'd been to Le Cordon Bleu. I believe you even had your chef coat on when you arrived for the first time. *And* you knew what you wanted to do—you even had the name. You didn't come in there with a polished business plan, but you had the idea and the skills, and the question was whether or not I could help you turn it into a business. And I had a pretty firm belief it could be done. So that started the journey for us.

Laura: You listened and you didn't judge me—and that was a great feeling. I was so excited I had found the right person to help me.

Andrew: As we moved forward, I was surprised because I started to feel the same runaround that you were always getting. I remember we went to talk to one disabled self-employment program, and when you said you wanted help starting your own restaurant, they tried to place you as an employee in somebody else's bakery. How many times did they ask you?

Laura: Oh, a lot, actually. And I just kept telling them no.

Andrew: And then, when we had to submit your business plan for review, I noticed that it was taking quite a bit of time. A lot of business development grants, you would be amazed at how quickly they can fly through. But virtually anybody who had an idea at any level would bounce it back to us, asking for multiple, multiple revisions.

We worked for about a year and a half together, and we were very close to getting the plan approved. And then I had a disagreement with the executive director of my organization, and that was the end of my job.

Laura: I was crushed when you told me—I think I even cried. Nobody there called me; nobody said *anything*. But you kept helping me.

Andrew: Well, it was like we were fighting in the ring together at that point, right? It was not only important for you, but for me, too.

There was probably three or four months when I was unemployed, and we would continue to look at restaurant spaces together. And it was very touching, because you were always trying to buy me coffee or give me money for gas.

But then I was offered a job. And I don't know if I told you this, Chef. But during my first interview for the position, I said, "I have this one client," and I told them your story. I said, "We've been working together for a year and a half. And I need to finish this." And they were very supportive.

And then, suddenly, about six months ago, things started to speed up pretty quickly. And we *finally* got approval.

Laura: Yeah. You called and you were excited, but you said to me, "You don't sound too happy." I was, but I was also in shock. La Diosa is my first restaurant, and it's like my baby; it's a great responsibility, and I put the best of me in it. And if it wasn't for you, I would probably still be out there with only half of my dream.

Andrew: Actually, I disagree. I am very happy I got the opportunity to help you, but you are *very* determined. It's been an honor to work with you.

Laura: I think our bond is beyond adviser or a client. I mean, I think we've built a great friendship.

Andrew: You're a pioneer, Chef. You're a groundbreaker.

RECORDED IN CHICAGO, ILLINOIS, ON FEBRUARY 4, 2015.

FORD ASSEMBLY PLANT SUPERVISOR DOROTHY GLINTON, 64, TALKS TO HER SON, SONARI GLINTON, 33.

Dorothy Glinton: My first job was in high school in Miami. I was living there with my aunt and uncle. During that time the city was real touristy and had lots of cafeterias, and so after school I was a salad girl at this place on Miami Beach. I always wanted to go to college, so all through high school I was saving money—I think I made something like thirty-five dollars a week in tips. When I graduated and was ready to go to school, I asked my aunt about my money for the college, but she said that she didn't have it. She told me that she had used it for us to live off of because my uncle was out of work. And that kind of broke my heart.

So I just got married, although that really was not what I wanted to do. And I kept working, doing odd jobs and working in nursing homes and in restaurants, but I didn't want to spend my whole life working as a domestic. And so after two years, I separated from my husband and went to Chicago with nothing but my baby—your sister, Alison—and my clothes. I wanted something different for me and my child, and I thought I would have better opportunities there. I wanted to go to school, but that didn't happen right away. When I got to Chicago, I put college on the back burner to make a living.

I got a job. I went to GTE—General Telephone and Electric. I stayed there for six years, but I got laid off. So in '72 I applied for college.

GTE actually called me back to work, but by that time I had gotten accepted in college—and I didn't ever want to come back to that job. My friends thought I had lost my mind. One of my girlfriends begged me not to quit. She said, "How are you going to take care of a kid if you leave this job?" But I told her, I said, "In September I'm leaving. I'm going to school." And that's the way I did it.

Sonari Glinton: So you were thirty when you started going to college. What was that like?

Dorothy: It was awful. During that time, I also had you, and I just felt like I was never, ever prepared. I had to study extremely hard and maintain an apartment, clothes, tuition, a babysitter. All of that made it really difficult for me. But that's what drove me to drive *you*—to make sure that you was prepared, and that you could compete with anybody.

I got through it, and I graduated in June of '76, when you were two years old. The whole time I was in school, I worked in this little liquor store in Hyde Park making $125 a week and did work-study jobs on campus. One of the clerks in the store had quit and got a job at Ford, and she brought her check into the store for me to cash. When I saw her check, I said, "What kind of job you got, making this kind of money?" [Laughs.]

I never will forget it: $502 she brought home in one week. I said, "You've got to be kidding!" That was more than I made in a month! I could pay my kids' tuition, I could fill a freezer up, I wouldn't have to worry about the lights, the rent, nothing.

I didn't want to work on the assembly line, but I needed the money, and I thought, *I could do anything for a few months.* But when I got to Ford it was so hard. I said, *Lord, I've got to find a job that I can do for thirty years in this place.* I had to find a job that I could use my skills and my education; I had to do something different.

So one morning, I put my blue suit on and my little white blouse, and I went to the corporate office and asked to see the plant manager. I wanted to know, why didn't they have any women in management, and if I was qualified—which I was— why couldn't they hire me? He was shocked, but he said, "Okay." So I applied for a job in management, took a few tests, and passed. I believe I was the second woman to go into management at the Chicago plant. I thought I just had it made, but that's when the crap really hit the fan.

The guys felt like us women were taking men's jobs. They'd do all kinds of practical jokes, like the time I found a mouse in a bucket near my desk, or they'd put ball bearing grease on my phone. One of them would open his toolbox and have all these naked pictures of women in there. They would display these gross pictures just to shock me, so I acted like I didn't even see them.

And you could never complain. I was there eight years before I missed a day, because I was afraid to take off. I just didn't want to make it harder for me.

They said I needed to spend more time with people. But on my lunch, I was more concerned about who could help me with a babysitter. We worked long hours. I'd get off at four o'clock in the morning; then I'd come get you, cook breakfast, drop you and your sister off to school; then I'd go to bed, and start all over again, ripping and running. I had a full plate—I couldn't stay in the parking lot and talk to the fellas, and drink beer and bond with them. I had stuff to do.

I had two kids, and I wanted the things for you that I didn't have. You know, money isn't everything, but money made it possible for you to go to good schools—to go to college—and that's what I wanted for you. So I just endured.

Sonari: Did it get better?

Dorothy: It got better in the sense that there were more of us in management and we stuck together. Ford was a good company, but I felt like if I just stood there and did not try to make things better when I saw other people having the same problems I was having, everything would be in vain. There was not one white male who was in my position and stayed in the same position for twenty years with the education that I had. It just wasn't fair. So we sued Ford for the way they were treating us.

People thought I was crazy. They said, "You can't go up against one of the Big Three!" But we did, and a lot changed: we have women superintendents, women area managers, women plant managers, women in overseas operation. I did

 what I did so that it would be better for the people coming behind me. And I believe I did make that difference.

RECORDED IN CHICAGO, ILLINOIS, ON JUNE 30, 2007.

FRANK SCOTT, 67, REMEMBERS HIS FATHER, NASCAR DRIVER WENDELL SCOTT, WITH HIS SON, WARRICK SCOTT, 37.

Frank Scott: My father, Wendell Scott, started racing cars in 1952. And once he got into NASCAR, that was it—he was racing 365 days a year. He was like Picasso in that car—a great artist doing his work.

As children, we didn't have leisure time. He said to us, "I need you in the garage." We had to be there because he was working twenty-four hours a day, seven days a week. I started working there at age seven, washing tools, learning what the numbers on the wrenches meant.

But the shop was also like a community center. It was a place that the locals that worked in the tobacco factories or down in the mills would come to when they got off work, because the shop never closed. In the summertime they'd come by to get a slice of cold watermelon and cantaloupe that my father kept, and in the wintertime they'd get a bologna sandwich. There was always a group of people there, just because of the excitement of us working on the race cars.

Warrick Scott: Were there other black NASCAR drivers at that time?

Frank: No, none. He wasn't allowed to race at certain speedways. He had death threats not to come to Atlanta. He said, "If I leave in a pine box, that's what I got to do, but I'm going to race."

I can remember him racing in Jacksonville, and he beat them all. But they wouldn't drop the checkered flag. And when they did drop the flag, they had my father in third place. One of the reasons that they gave was that there was a white beauty queen who always kissed the driver, and they said it would cause a race riot. Daddy said, "Look, all I want is my money and my trophy."

He had three things that he always had to be concerned about on tour. First, where to get a warm meal. Every seventy-five, one hundred miles, there may have been a truck stop, but he couldn't go in. Or he had to go through the back door. Second, a lot of times he couldn't find hotels to stay in. Sometimes he had to sleep on picnic tables or on the ground—or in the race car. And then he knew he had to have extra gas in a can, because all the truck stops were white only.

Warrick: Did he ever consider not racing anymore?

Frank: Never. Even when he was in his sixties. I mean, I can remember him getting injured, and he would just take a handful of axle grease and put it in the cut and keep working. He used to say, "When it's too tough for everybody else, it's just right for me."

I remember when we were racing the Atlanta 500 and my father was sick. He had an ulcerated stomach. I said, "Daddy, we don't have to race today." He whispered to me, "Lift my legs up and put me in the car." Whenever he told you something, he didn't want to tell you twice. So I took my arm and put it behind his legs, and I lifted him into the car. He drove five hundred miles that day.

Later that night, when we were alone, he apologized. He said, "I know I frightened you today, but I knew that once I got in the seat, I'd be all right."

Warrick: How did his racing career officially end?

Frank: Finances. He couldn't get the support. The drivers that we were competing against had major sponsorships. The automobile companies would provide them as many cars as they needed, engineers, technical advice, everything. Daddy did everything on his own, basically just having to operate on a shoestring budget. Parts that someone else threw away—he'd take them and make them work. Even if he had a real big night, he never could have the luxuries that went along with being successful. Everything he won had to go back into the car and taking care of the family.

My father passed away in 1990, and I think of him every single day of my life. Every day. When I'm working on cars, which I like to do, and I run into a situation that's kind of difficult, I say, "OK, Daddy, what should I do?"

Two words we were never allowed to use in our household was *can't* and *never*. If you did, you immediately got his attention. He told people, "Man, you can't? Get out my damn garage, and come back when you get your head right." And everywhere I've ever been, I've taken that with me.

He always felt like someday he was going to get his big break. He said, "One day they're going to write a book about me." But for twenty years, nobody mentioned Wendell Scott. At one point it was like he never existed. But see, he didn't let

it drive him crazy. I think that's what made him so great.

RECORDED IN DANVILLE, VIRGINIA, ON JANUARY 10, 2015.

On January 30, 2015, Wendell Scott became the first African American to be inducted into the NASCAR Hall of Fame.

BUILDING CONTRACTOR
LYLE LINK, 90, TALKS TO
HIS GRANDDAUGHTER
CARLY DREHER, 24.

Lyle Link: I grew up on a dairy farm in southern Waukesha County. My father believed that any man that needed a vacation should get a different job—because for him, those 147 acres was the whole world, and he needed nothing else.

My brother was the good son, because he never questioned; he just did. He was a total farmer, and never made a footstep that my father hadn't made before. But I was the bad son; I couldn't walk in my father's footsteps to save my soul.

Farming just wasn't for me, and I drove my poor father nuts. He couldn't understand me. He said to me one day, "Son, you cannot think the thoughts you think." I dropped out of high school because I thought I was smarter than the teachers, which was of course not true. I'm ninety years old, and I'm still making up for it. But I always thought way too big for my britches. I just wasn't happy where I was; if I heard a train whistle, I wanted to go with that train every time.

Well, the day came, and I left town. Your grandma and I had six kids at that point. I thought I was going to work for a friend in the construction business, but it turned out he didn't have one. And so suddenly I had to be a contractor and I didn't know how.

Carly Dreher: So what was that like then?

Lyle: I was overwhelmed, but I don't think I was scared. I had so much chutzpah that I could bluff my way through. Every problem has a solution if you know where to look, and if you don't get too panicked. I had a characteristic that was a saving grace: I had a natural ability to find an answer before I worked out the problem. I could make a judgment and it would be so near correct that the customer didn't know that I didn't know what I was talking about. That's the characteristic of a very good salesman. So apparently what I really was, was a salesman. And that's the reason I wasn't happy shucking corn or shoveling manure or milking a cow.

After the long depression and the war, the country had money to spend, and there was an *unconscionable* amount of profit in the building business—the sky was the limit. It was easy to be a success, but it was even easier to be a rich man if you were dishonest. Well, the upbringing that I had didn't allow for that. I did everything in my power to show people that

I could be trusted. When you build a building, you don't build it to just have it fall down in a couple of years. A building is a monument, it's built to last, and that's what I wanted to do. I lived that to the nth degree—and it worked.

For twenty-five years I worked without a contract; I just used the old-fashioned trust of a handshake. I would do million-dollar jobs that were drawn on the back of a napkin in a restaurant where we were talking, and that would be the extent of the plan.

Carly: Do you have any regrets, Grandpa?

Lyle: No, it was a wonderful life. And it's hard for me to remember that I ever worked. Successes don't teach you much, but mistakes? That's a learning situation. I made a lot of mistakes, but I learned a lot because I did. I couldn't afford to get too scared—and I want you to do the same thing. Live with courage.

RECORDED IN MILWAUKEE, WISCONSIN, ON DECEMBER 22, 2007.

Lyle Link passed away on April 25, 2010.

ACKNOWLEDGMENTS

This book was pulled together with skill, grace, and heart by Maya Millett, who is blessed with the magic touch. Her work throughout was overseen and aided by Lizzie Jacobs, who, among other roles, is the executive editor of print projects at StoryCorps. Makeba Rasin and Cailey Cron of the print team were also instrumental in bringing *Callings* to life. Additional thanks to Ryan Salim, Kelly Shetron, Emily Hsiao, Xandra Clark, Cassandra Lizaire, Angeline Rodriguez, and Felix Lopez. Gratitude to researcher and fact-checker Mitra Bonshahi, with additional fact-checking from Julie Schwietert Collazo and Regan Hofmann. Thanks for editorial assistance from Anne Ford, photo-retouching from Randy Reed, and flawless transcriptions from the Audio Transcription Company. For additional editorial insight and input, profound gratitude to Donna Galeno, Kathrina Proscia, Robin Sparkman, and Jane Isay.

We feel blessed to have a home at the Penguin Press. Thanks to our longtime publisher, editor, cheerleader, and friend, Scott Moyers. Thanks also to the incomparable Ann Godoff, for allowing us to put out our *fifth* StoryCorps book with the best publishers in the business. Profound gratitude to Liz Calamari and Meghan White, also at Penguin. Thanks always to our one-of-a-kind agent, David Black, who has our back 24-7.

Gratitude to our friends and family at NPR, the Library of Congress, and the hundreds of other national and local partners and public radio stations we work closely with year in and year out. Special thanks to our generous funders, donors, and sponsors who make everything we do possible. Boundless thanks to Gara LaMarche and the StoryCorps Board—and, of course, to our magnificent, profoundly committed, and brilliant staff who bring StoryCorps to life each day.

FAVORITE STORYCORPS QUESTIONS

- What was the happiest moment of your life? The saddest?
- Who has been the most important person in your life? Can you tell me about him or her?
- What lessons has your work life taught you?
- What are you proudest of in your life?
- Are there any words of wisdom you'd like to pass along to me?
- How has your life been different than what you'd imagined?
- How would you like to be remembered?
- Do you have any regrets?
- Is there anything that you've never told me but want to tell me now?
- Is there something about me that you've always wanted to know but have never asked?

CONTINUE THE CONVERSATION

Visit www.storycorps.org to

- support StoryCorps;
- listen to more stories and share them with others;
- view our animated shorts;
- subscribe to our podcast;
- find out where our booths are located and how to bring StoryCorps to your community; and
- check out StoryCorpsU, our college-readiness curriculum, as well as other resources for educators.

Download the StoryCorps app to

- record StoryCorps interviews any time, any place with your mobile device and upload your conversations with one tap to the American Folklife Center at the Library of Congress; and
- browse and listen to stories from other users.

One hundred percent of the royalties from this book will be donated to StoryCorps, a not-for-profit organization.

Lead funding for StoryCorps comes from the Corporation for Public Broadcasting.

Lead corporate funding for StoryCorps comes from Cancer Treatment Centers of America and Subaru of America.

Major funders include Airbnb, the Arcus Foundation, the Bill & Melinda Gates Foundation, the Einhorn Family Charitable Trust, the Ford Foundation, the Institute of Museum and Library Services, the John D. and Catherine T. MacArthur Foundation, the John S. and James L. Knight Foundation, the Kaplen Brothers Fund, the Marc Haas Foundation, and the W.K. Kellogg Foundation, as well as Joe and Carol Reich.

Additional funders include the Baytree Fund, Bloomberg Philanthropies, the Boeing Company, the Chicago Community Trust, the Joyce Foundation, the National Endowment for the Arts, the New York City Department of Cultural Affairs, and the Robert Sterling Clark Foundation.

Legal services are generously donated by Latham & Watkins and Holland & Knight.

For a complete and current list of all of our supporters, please visit our website: www.storycorps.org.

National partners include the Smithsonian National Museum of African American History and Culture, the National September 11 Memorial & Museum, the American Folklife Center, National Public Radio, PBS, and POV.

ABOUT THE AUTHORS

Dave Isay is the founder of StoryCorps and the recipient of broadcasting honors that include numerous Peabody Awards, a MacArthur "Genius" Fellowship, and the 2015 TED Prize.

He is the author and editor of numerous books that grew out of his public radio documentary work, including the StoryCorps books *Listening Is an Act of Love* (2007), *Mom: A Celebration of Mothers from StoryCorps* (2010), and *All There Is: Love Stories from StoryCorps* (2012)—all *New York Times* bestsellers. StoryCorps' fourth book, *Ties That Bind: Stories of Love & Gratitude from the First Ten Years of StoryCorps*, was released in the fall of 2013 to coincide with the organization's tenth anniversary.

Maya Millett is a writer and editor living in Brooklyn. She received a master's degree in journalism from New York University, where she studied cultural reporting and criticism. Before joining StoryCorps' print department in 2010, Maya worked as an archive researcher for Johnson Publishing Company (home to *Ebony* and *Jet* magazines) and with the African American oral history project The HistoryMakers.